SOCIAL WORKERS AND VOLUNTEERS

Social Workers and Volunteers

ANTHEA HOLME and JOAN MAIZELS

GEORGE ALLEN & UNWIN
BRITISH ASSOCIATION OF SOCIAL WORKERS

First published in 1978

ISBN 0-04-361031-5 Hardback
      0-04-361032-3 Paperback

British Library Cataloguing in Publication Data

Holme, Anthea
    Social workers and volunteers.
    1. Volunteer workers in social service —
    Great Britain
    I. Title   II. Maizels, Joan   III. British
    Association of Social Workers
    361.7′0941   HV245   78-40012

    ISBN 0-04-361031-5
    ISBN 0-04-361032-3   Pbk

George Allen & Unwin (Publishers) Ltd, 40 Museum Street,
London WC1A 1LU

British Association of Social Workers, 16 Kent Street,
Birmingham B5 6RD

Photoset in 10 on 11 point English Times
by Red Lion Setters, Holborn, London.

Printed in Great Britain by
Unwin Brothers Limited, Old Woking, Surrey

Note on the Funding Bodies and the Steering Committee

The project was generously financed by the Leverhulme Trust, the King Edward's Hospital Fund and the City Parochial Foundation. The grants were administered on behalf of BASW by the Social Workers' Educational Trust, a registered charity set up in 1972. Responsibility for the Project was vested in the Association's Professional Development and Practice Committee which appointed a Steering Committee composed of the following members:

Foreword

One of the most striking features of the 1960s was the revival of individual voluntary action. A long-standing tradition was injected with fresh energy and conviction. With its concern to enlist community participation in the development of the personal social services, the Seebohm Committee reflected the prevalent mood. Hopes were aroused that the proposed social services departments would become vehicles for involving volunteers. The Probation and After-Care Service had already begun to demonstrate some of the possibilities as a new generation of volunteers took part with probation officers in revitalising services for prisoners and their families.

The Report of the Aves Committee, *The Voluntary Worker in the Social Services*, published in 1969, was, therefore, well timed both to comment upon the events of the preceding decade and to look forward to new opportunities in the restructured health and social services. Central to effective partnership between statutory and voluntary service lay the willingness and ability of individual professionals and volunteers to work together, but the Committee had received evidence of tension and of a tendency for each to adopt critical stereotypes of the other. Plainly the relationship between professionals and volunteers was a key area for future investigation and the need for this in the social work field was quickly recognised.

The present research grew out of discussions within the British Association of Social Workers following the publication of the Aves Report and reflected its concerns. This book, based upon a representative national sample, provides for the first time systematic evidence of the degree to which social workers engage the help of volunteers and of their attitudes towards them. Within the resources available, regrettably, it was not possible to carry out parallel surveys recording the experience and views of volunteers and clients, but the present findings provide pointers for future studies from these perspectives. Nor has the survey attempted to evaluate the volunteers' contribution save in so far as reference is made to social workers' opinions.

The findings of this inquiry indicate that the numbers of volunteers throughout the United Kingdom are not insubstantial and that the majority of social workers either do involve or have involved them. None the less, the number working with social workers at any given time is small, relative to the size of the social workers' total workload.

During a period of constraint on public expenditure, the case for relying more on voluntary effort may be presented as a political imperative. However, from the evidence of this survey, involving volunteers offers no panacea for the cash crisis in the personal social services. Those who are predisposed to exhort social workers to enlist the help of more volunteers should find the researchers' conclusions especially pertinent. If, as is suggested, organisational constraints rather than professional attitudes limit the involvement of volunteers, then any significant increase in their numbers may only be possible in the context of fundamental changes in agency structure and in the redefinition of the relationships with the communities that they serve. The appointment of voluntary help organisers alone, according to the survey, is unlikely to lead to more than a slight increase in the number of social workers who involve volunteers.

There is, however, much in the survey upon which advocates of increased participation and social workers will want to reflect. Why, for example, are volunteers typically excluded from those situations commonly described as 'casework'? This may be answered either in terms of the social workers' view of their professional skills, or by virtue of the fact that those skills are most frequently applied to client groups who may be seen to be especially vulnerable and/or subject to statutory provisions. As a result, social workers may be reluctant to relinquish personal responsibility. Whatever the explanations, cogent arguments can be advanced for involving volunteers more often with, for example, children at risk and the mentally ill, and for examining the implications that this would carry for closer partnership between social workers and volunteers.

However, the findings also suggest that volunteers are most often involved with those client groups with whom many social workers least prefer to work. By the same token, those client groups are often passed 'down the line' to unqualified social workers and, more particularly, social work assistants. Thus, even where the paid and voluntary workers are in regular contact, the chances of the latter having the support and advice of qualified social workers is remote. One way, in the short term, to obviate this problem would be to use qualified social workers as consultants to groups of volunteers. In the longer term, increases in the proportion of social workers who are qualified, and perhaps changes in the allocation of cases, may serve to bring individual volunteers and qualified social workers into more frequent contact.

These issues take on a particularly interesting form in the light of the comparisons made in this report between the ways in which probation and after-care services and social services departments relate to volunteers. The authors suggest that the former typically adopt a 'complementary model' and the latter a 'supplementary model'. The complementary model, by definition, provides for a closer working relationship between social workers and volunteers. Moreover, probation and after-care services now have predominantly qualified probation officers. This suggests that social services departments may have something to learn from probation and after-care services about the ways in which qualified social workers and volunteers could work together more closely and more frequently. Equally, probation and after-care services might learn from the experience of social services departments. The supplementary model provides a looser contact with a network of voluntary help within the community, help that may not be forthcoming on a more formal and regulated basis. Might there not be advantages if probation and after-care services could tap the same network on a collaborative basis? The validity of these models, and the extent to which they illuminate differences between these two major statutory services, emerge as central topics.

These are just some of the issues presented by the findings of this survey. How then do they relate to wider issues? Much attention for example is now being paid to staffing patterns in the personal social services. Determined efforts are being made to identify and develop the distinctive skills of particular occupational groups, to provide the training that they require and to ensure that skilled personnel are used to optimum effect. It is within this context that we may be able to look further at the contribution of volunteers, not as a homogeneous group but as individuals who can contribute a rich and diverse range of talents. Thus a variety of professionals and a variety of volunteers may come to comprise the multipurpose team. Such a vision goes beyond the present survey, but merits study if the findings of this research are to be related to current issues regarding staffing policies.

During the long gestation between its conception and eventual publication, any research project runs the risk of being overtaken by events. On this occasion, nothing could be further from the case. The Steering Committee is, therefore, able to commend the report as a timely contribution to the continuing debate about the place of the volunteer in the development of manpower policies for the personal social services.

October 1977   HUGH BARR,
                                                  for the Steering Committee

Acknowledgements

This inquiry was made possible by the advice, help and co-operation of many people. There are first, the social workers who took part in the pilot and main studies, and the directors and chief probation officers of the authorities concerned, on whom the success of the project depended. Then there are all those who generously gave their time during the exploratory stages of the study and helped, through their discussions with us, to clarify the main areas of inquiry. Finally, there are those, and especially the members of our Steering Committee, who supported and encouraged us in various ways throughout the three years of the study. To each and all we extend our warmest thanks.

We should like to acknowledge a particular debt of gratitude to our Research Assistant, Judith Nasatyr, who contributed so much to the content as well as to the organisation of the study, and to all our other helpers, notably, Gloria Moleman, Pat Katterhorn and Kay Allen; to Joan Baraclough and Hugh Barr for their continued and valued assistance and counsel; to June Neill for her valuable ideas and comments; to those whose technical advice was crucial to the implementation of the project and in the analysis of the data—Louis Moss, our Research Consultant; Jean Morton-Williams and Dave Walker of Social and Community Planning Research for organising the data processing; Eileen Goddard for advising on the sample, and Alfred Maizels for undertaking the regression analysis; and finally to those—particularly Christopher Holme and again Alfred Maizels—whose suggestions helped to improve the text and the tables.

We should also like to say how happily we worked at the National Institute for Social Work with the use of its extensive facilities, and to acknowledge the friendly and helpful co-operation of the then Director—Tilda Goldberg—and the staff of its Research Department.

Note on Terminology

In this study, the term *social workers* excludes occupational therapists, home help organisers and others providing similar social services, but includes social work assistants and trainees. In the analysis of the data these two designations are distinguished. When discussing social work staff in general terms, however, they are, unless otherwise stated, included in our references to *social workers* or the *social work sample*. Similarly, the terms *social workers, the social work sample*, or *the social work profession* include, unless otherwise stated, both qualified and unqualified workers.

Furthermore, throughout the study, basic-grade social workers—described in the Department of Health and Social Security (DHSS) Returns (1974) as *other social workers*—are referred to as *fieldworkers*. This, of course, in no way implies that other practitioners in more senior or, in the case of assistants and trainees, more junior ranks are not also working in the field.

One further point of clarification is necessary. *The social work profession* or *social workers*, in our terminology, naturally include members of the probation service—or, more correctly, the Probation and After-Care Service. When, however, it is necessary to distinguish between the two services in the study, members of the one are described as *local authority social workers* and of the other as *probation officers*.

Contents

1 Introducing the Study

BACKGROUND AND AIMS

Social work today relies on a work force of paid and unpaid labour—the 'professionals' and the 'volunteers'. For social work, however, these terms, and the functions they represent, belong only to modern times. Formerly, the field of action of a volunteer would have been the army, and social work as a profession did not exist. We often hear today of the role of the volunteer as 'traditional', rooted in past history. Yet this idea itself is actually of recent origin. The numerous activities undertaken in the last and present centuries by those moved by charity, philanthropy or social reform became distinctively 'voluntary' only as the necessity grew for increasing state intervention in education, health, industrial and social welfare, and the personal social services.

Moreover, the individuals who in former days carried out voluntarily what we now call social work had little in common with today's professional social workers. Their background and skills differed. The tasks undertaken in earlier times were not like those falling within the province of today's social worker. More important, the earlier well-doers were not regarded as *volunteers* either by themselves or others, whatever the manner in which they approached the task on hand. This is well documented in the novels of the time—a unique source of social observation. Charlotte Brontë's Shirley Keeldar for example, saw herself, if somewhat ironically, as meeting her obligations by easing her 'lord-of-the-manor' conscience through the medium of 'good works' (Brontë, 1849). Mrs Gaskell's heroine, Margaret Hale, unselfconsciously committed herself to a relationship of deep affection with the young Bessie, which withstood the inequalities of social position and the conflicts arising from industrial unrest (Gaskell, 1854).

Only with the rise of the social work profession did the distinctive titles of *voluntary worker* or *volunteer* come to be used. Precisely when we do not know, but to a growing extent it served to differentiate the professional and paid from the voluntary and unpaid social worker, and to demarcate their respective spheres of influence. In more recent years, both professionals and volunteers have been equally concerned to develop a new image and to break with the past.

This study began in 1974 at a time when the respective contribution of the professional and the volunteer in social work was the subject of fresh concern. Social work was beginning to assume a new professional identity, largely as a result of a rapid growth in the numbers of social workers employed in the statutory sector, which itself had only recently been reorganised and charged with new obligations and responsibilities. There had been a revival of interest in volunteers, and concern expressed that their 'traditional role' should be safeguarded and their continuing contribution ensured, whatever the changes in the statutory services.

In addition the growth of voluntary work during the twenty years or so preceding reorganisation had been slowest in those social services, where the place of the professional social worker was most clearly established (Aves, 1969). Perhaps this was one of the reasons that the Seebohm Committee (1968), in its proposals for the reorganisation of local authority personal social services, stressed the need 'to enlist the help of large numbers of volunteers to complement the teams of professional workers'. Morris (1969) also argued at the time that the contribution of the voluntary worker was an integral part of any restructuring of the social services. In the view of the Aves Committee, too, the most fruitful use of volunteers in the social services was as 'an extension of and complement to the work of qualified staff'.

Clearly then, the hope was that, as the social services expanded following reorganisation, so would there be greater recruitment of volunteers. Working alongside the professional social workers, they would become involved in increasing numbers in an ever widening range of activities.

The present inquiry is an outcome of these developments and of the interest stimulated by publication of the Aves Committee Report. It is a first attempt to fill some of the gaps which this Report revealed. When our inquiry began there was no information about the scale on which professional social workers were working with volunteers, the nature of their mutual relationships, or the types of activity in which they were engaged.

The whole topic was central to the interests and responsibilities of the newly formed British Association of Social Workers (BASW). As a result of discussions between interested individuals, a three-year research project under the sponsorship of BASW was eventually devised. The main research aims of the study were to discover:

(1)   the extent to which social workers used volunteers, the nature of their relationships with them, and the types of activity in which they were engaged;
(2)   how social workers themselves perceived the role and contribution of volunteers, and their assessment of their experiences, if any, of working with them;
(3)   some of the factors which were significantly associated with the use of volunteers.

In brief, it was hoped to find out how things stood with the professional and the voluntary worker in the personal social services; to provide some possible explanations for the facts revealed and so to extend understanding of the various issues involved.

This book is an account of the findings of our study. Their implications for policy and practice, however, need to be considered in the light of recent events. By 1977—the time of writing—a new set of influences due to the instability of world economic conditions and their special impact on Britain had come into play. Almost every sphere of social provision has been cut back or run down. What seemed only a short while ago to be a rapid development of an assured area of professional influence has been drastically arrested. At the same time, interest in the voluntary contribution has again grown, and the use of volunteers is increasingly canvassed to sustain or even to replace professional activities.

This turn of events prompts two observations. First, the roles of the professional and the volunteer in social work cannot be defined without reference to each other. This interdependence is such that any change in the scope and function of the one affects those of the other. Secondly, there are no fixed or settled roles for either. Their respective scope and function are subject to change according to circumstances largely beyond their control, so that any division of labour between them may be regarded as transient, related only to the particular circumstances of the time. This book should be read, therefore, with these considerations in mind.

METHOD OF INQUIRY

The present inquiry represented a new field of investigation, since little relevant data on the subject were previously available. For this reason, and because the main instrument of investigation was to be a postal questionnaire, we attached great importance to the preparatory work and gave it particular care.

This preparatory phase had four main objectives: first, to gather together ideas about current developments and practices; secondly, to discover how the topic of study was generally regarded, and the meaning it had for the various people concerned; thirdly to establish a basis for some working hypotheses, and fourthly, to clarify the kinds of research problems posed by the inquiry, and thus to lay the foundations for the more systematic questioning to follow.

The main technique used for the development of ideas in all these respects was to meet and talk on progressively more structured lines, with individuals and groups working at different levels of the personal social services. The range of people seen included new recruits to social work, students in training, fieldworkers, senior and management staff, teachers of social work and those engaged in research.

It was apparent from these discussions that the main theme of the study—the relationships between professionals and volunteers—was thought to be important and useful, though complex. Its complexity was accentuated by the fact that the terms *social worker* and *volunteer* appeared to have somewhat different meanings for those engaged in social work, depending for example, on the nature of their commitments to different social work methods, particularly if these commitments extended to community-centred developments. There were also more deep-seated problems from which it seemed that the research topic could not be dissociated. These were mainly attributed to changes in the organisation of the social services and in the nature of the obligations which these services were expected to discharge. Indeed, important as the subject of voluntary activity was thought to be, it was still in most people's minds peripheral to what were considered the more basic problems—those relating to the roles and tasks of the professionals themselves.

Thus social workers' anxieties and frustrations concerning their roles, identities and methods of work, and their references to the blurring of boundaries and the undermining of their professionalism were frequent themes in our discussions. At the same time, it seemed that attitudes and expectations fluctuated considerably. The organisational framework, the characteristics of the work setting, and the interactions of different structural elements were emphasised as being important in producing the stresses or satisfactions which often influence actual behaviour.

We became increasingly convinced that a considerable knowledge and understanding of the underlying relationship between professionals and volunteers could be gained through intensive study of some of the different situations to be found in the social services today. There appeared to be marked differences in the nature and quality of the involvement of volunteers in social work and with social workers, as there were in their patterns of social interaction. We came to believe, moreover, that the use of volunteers in different ways might be associated at one level with deep feelings, not always clearly articulated or explicit. These may be related to the capacity to share what is precious, meaningful and satisfying in the social worker's daily activity, as well as to the client's perceived needs for long-term or short-term supportive relationships. Such a study was inconsistent with the original brief, however, nor would resources of time and money have permitted the use both of intensive and of extensive methods of inquiry.

The extensive methods finally adopted for the study resulted in findings from which generalisations could be made—one aim in setting up the project. Moreover, the insights gained as a result of the preparatory discussions gave meaning to the broader factual picture provided by the main survey, and allowed the implications of the involvement of volunteers for social work practice to be more fully assessed.

At the end of this preparatory phase, though we were not able to fit our ideas into any one coherent theory, we were ready to formulate some working hypotheses. These centred on four main areas which seemed to us at the time as possibly related to the use of volunteers. These were: first, the size and composition of social workers' caseloads and the nature of the work they generated; secondly, certain aspects of caseload management; thirdly, the social workers' individual backgrounds, personal attributes, experience and training in social work; and fourthly, their satisfaction or otherwise with their work roles which, as seemed evident from the exploratory discussions, was among the main preoccupations of social workers. In the event, these last two factors proved to be less directly relevant to volunteer use than those associated with the social worker's task.

Questions were then prepared and tested—first in interviews with the staff of two area offices, and then in a pilot exercise.

The Pilot Study

The pilot study was designed as much to test the response of social workers as to test the design of the questionnaire. It also made possible the assessment of the representativeness of different groups of social workers covered by such a postal survey. Two main sources of respondents were used. These were the social work staff of fifteen area offices in local authority social services and social work departments in England and Scotland, and the members of three BASW branches, one of which was in Northern Ireland. We thought that different methods of approach might influence the response. Hence, in the local authority areas we adopted a personal approach. In almost all instances we met the directors, senior management and some senior staff. In some instances, we met all or some of the social workers who would be receiving the questionnaire. There was no personal contact with members of the BASW branches. We also used two versions of the questionnaire—a longer and a shorter—dispatching 443 in all.

Four important questions were resolved as a result of the response of social workers to the pilot questionnaire. First, the response rate itself—62 per cent of those holding caseloads—was considered satisfactory enough for a postal questionnaire (in its longer version) to be adopted as the main research instrument. Secondly, it was evident that a representative sample of social workers could be obtained only from local authority social services departments. Thirdly, it appeared that some prior personal contact was helpful in achieving a satisfactory response. Fourthly, the replies showed that in the main study it would be necessary to distinguish social workers according to whether they had formerly used volunteers or had never done so or, if currently using them, according to whether or not the volunteers in question worked directly under their guidance.

The Main Sample

It was clear that, if inferences for the social worker population as a whole were to be drawn from the main study results, a sample of at least 2,000 social workers would need to be approached. Three considerations influenced the choice of a sampling frame. Firstly, there should be national coverage, making possible a representative selection of authorities.[1] Secondly, those approached should be people whose work gave them, in one way or another, the opportunity of using the services of volunteers.[2] Thirdly, the work setting and the nature of the caseloads should be sufficiently alike to allow for the use of one common questionnaire. This last consideration regrettably disqualified residential social workers and those working in day centres, sheltered workshops and similar establishments, and also professional social workers in local authority departments other than those of the social services.

It had been hoped to include social workers from the voluntary agencies, but the formidable difficulties of drawing a representative sample forced us in the end to exclude them. However, a small survey, independent of the main study, was carried out, the results of which are summarised in Appendix I.

The probation service was another matter. Though the differences between this and the local authority services were recognised, we decided that these were not so great as to justify excluding probation officers from the inquiry. Moreover, the pilot questionnaire had been satisfactorily completed by probation officers, with a response rate of 78 per cent. There was also the important point that the use of volunteers in the probation service was known to be such as to make its inclusion extremely useful for comparative purposes.

Thus the total population from which the sample was to be drawn was to comprise social work staff based primarily in area offices of local authority social services departments in Great Britain, and in branch offices of the probation services in England and Wales. For the local authority services this amounted to some 19,000 individuals. It was decided to structure the sample on the basis of authorities, area offices and designations.[3] Out of twenty-six local authorities approached, twenty-one social services departments agreed to co-operate. Using lists supplied by these authorities, one in two social workers, stratified according to designation, were selected from each area office. This gave a total of 2,121 social workers to whom questionnaires were sent.[4]

The same administrative areas as those of the participating local authority social services departments (or the nearest equivalent where the boundaries did not coincide) were selected for the probation service. Again, our approach met with a positive response, only two areas finding it impossible to take part. This gave a total of well over 700 probation officers. In this instance, a selection of one in three individuals was made on the same principle and by the same methods as those used for the local authority services.

Two short supplementary questionnaires were also sent to all the area officers whose staff were taking part in the inquiry. It was hoped by these means to obtain background information without overburdening the individual social workers with more questions.[5]

All the questionnaires were distributed during the month of June 1975, with—where called for—two sets of follow-up reminders during July and August of that year.

THE RESPONSE AND THE REPRESENTATIVENESS OF THE SAMPLE

The use of a postal questionnaire as a method of data collection seems to be fully justified by the response achieved in the present inquiry. Three in five of the social workers and probation officers approached—1,423 in all—completed and returned their questionnaires within the time limit set.[6] The literature on postal surveys carried out in the last twenty years or so indicates that many resulted in a response rate as low as 20 per cent, while many others achieved a rate of 90 per cent. Experimental evidence has shown that there are many factors which may affect response—the presence or absence of certain questions, the nature of the sponsorship, the wording of the covering letter and so on—but none of these, according to Scott (1961), have been shown to have a large effect. Scott concluded that there was little reliable evidence about factors responsible for the variation in response rates.

It is possible, however, that in the present inquiry the rate of response may have been influenced in some degree by the length of the questionnaire and the amount of work its completion required. The response rate of 60 per cent was equivalent to that achieved in the pilot study. The response rate of local authority-based social workers was, however, marginally lower than that for the sample as a whole, being only 58 per cent. On this basis, the social worker sample represents just under one in twenty of the total social worker population of some 25,000 employed in local authority

Table 1.1 *Social workers and probation officers covered in present inquiry in relation to their total population in 1974*

Designation	Total social worker population[1]	Approached in present inquiry		Responding in present inquiry	
		Number	% of total population	Number	% of total population
Social workers					
Management and supervisory	5,312	456	8.6	319	6.0
Other social workers	15,005	1,322	8.8	694	4.6
Social work assistants	3,024	220	7.3	135	4.5
Trainees	1,954	122	6.2	72	3.7
TOTAL	25,295	2,120	8.4	1,220	4.8
Probation officers[2]	5,518	262	4.7	203	3.7

Sources: Social Service Staff, 1974 (S/F75/1), Statistics and Research Division, Department of Health and Social Security, 1975; Home Office estimates (for probation officers).

[1] Great Britain for social workers; England and Wales for probation officers.
[2] Including ancillaries.

social services departments in Great Britain, just under one in twelve of this total having been sent questionnaires (Table 1.1). The response rate of probation officers (79 per cent) was considerably higher than that of the local authority social workers. The sample of respondents represents fewer than one in twenty-five of all probation officers in England and Wales,[7] of whom only about one in twenty were asked to take part in the inquiry.

For social services department staff, response rates varied considerably among different authorities. (The probation officer sample was too small for local response rates to be distinguished.) In five local authority areas, two-thirds or more of the social workers participated in the inquiry. By contrast, in six other local authority areas, about one-half or fewer did so. Moreover, the response, on average, was higher from social workers working in metropolitan districts (70 per cent) than from those working in other types of local authority administrations, and lowest of all from the Scottish regions (Table 1.2).

We naturally wished to be assured that these response rates were high enough to give a sample which could be regarded as reasonably representative of the general social worker population. A comparison of the sex composition, age structure and job designation

Table 1.2   *Response to the inquiry according to type of local authority administration: local authority social workers*

Type of authority	Number	% response
Metropolitan districts	5	70
Outer London Boroughs	4	60
Counties	8	58
Inner London Boroughs	2	57
Scottish Regions	2	56
TOTAL	21	58

of the local authority social workers with the relevant DHSS returns for England 1974 showed a number of similarities. Women in the present inquiry, for example, predominate in almost the same ratio to men—three to two—as in the total social worker population (Table 1.3). The age structure of the social workers in the present sample also follows a similar pattern to that shown in the DHSS returns. The average age of respondents in the present inquiry is virtually the same as that for the social worker population as a whole (Table 1.4). Finally, in both populations, basic-grade social workers form the great majority (Table 1.5). The

Table 1.3   *Sex composition of sample of local authority social workers compared with DHSS returns*

	Present inquiry	DHSS returns[2]
	(% of total)	
Male	39	40
Female	61	60
TOTAL[1]	100	100
(number)	(1,054)	(18,219)

[1] Excludes social work assistants and trainee social workers.
[2] *Source:* Social Service Staff, 1974 (S/F75/1) Statistics and Research Division, Department of Health and Social Security, 1975 (England only).

proportionately higher numbers of social workers in the present inquiry who are in management and supervisory posts reflects the higher response of those groups.

It seemed important also to investigate the problem of non-response, particularly as those responding to the inquiry might have had a special interest in the subject and thus have been strongly motivated to reply. A comparative analysis of the gender, job designation and BASW membership of respondents and non-respondents showed that no serious bias had arisen on account of these characteristics. Similarly, the results of comparing the incidence of volunteer use among respondents according to the

Table 1.4   *Age structure of sample of local authority social workers compared with DHSS returns*

Present age (years)	Present inquiry	DHSS returns[2]
	(% of total)	
Under 25	11	11
25-34	37	34
35-54	43	45
Over 54	9	10
TOTAL[1]	100	100
(number)	(1,022)	(18,219)
Average age (*years*)	38.2	38.8

[1] Excludes social work assistants and trainee social workers.
[2] *Source:* Social Service Staff, 1974 (S/F75/1), Statistics and Research Division, Department of Health and Social Security, 1975.

Table 1.5   *Designations of sample of local authority social workers compared with DHSS returns*

Designation	Present inquiry	DHSS returns[2]
	(% of total)	
Management and supervisory	26	22[1]
Other social workers	57	58
Trainees	6	8
Social work assistants	11	12
TOTAL	100	100
(number)	(1,220)	(21,680)

[1] Including personnel employed in central social services department, *not* included in the present inquiry.
[2] *Source:* Social Service Staff, 1974 (S/F75/1), Statistics and Research Division, Department of Health and Social Security, 1975.

promptness of their return of the questionnaire, and estimating accordingly the proportion of non-respondents who might have been using volunteers, indicated that the degree of non-response did not introduce any important bias into the sample concerning the use of volunteers (the details of the analysis of response bias are given in Appendix II).

In the light of these various similarities, it is fair to assume that the results of the inquiry can be taken as reasonably representative of the social worker population as a whole.[8]

LIMITATIONS IN THE SCOPE OF THE INQUIRY

The findings described in the ensuing chapters relate exclusively to social workers' experiences and opinions, and then only to particular aspects of these. This means that the picture of voluntary help in the personal social services is by no means complete. There are important gaps.

The activities of volunteers, for example, have been described only in very broad terms and, since this description is derived from the accounts of social workers, it is not based on independent and first-hand observation. Nor does it take account of the client's point of view. No comparable information has been obtained from volunteers, so that their viewpoint, which may be considered as vital to a full understanding of the relationships between professionals and volunteers is missing. No information was obtained from directors of social services departments or from central office staff on the departments' policies concerning volunteers. Furthermore, our data cannot be placed in the context of the communities served by the local statutory services. Thus the possible influence of local history and traditions of voluntary effort, local developments, or environmental features—physical and demographic— cannot be assessed from the findings.

Furthermore, the research design used in the present inquiry gives rise to an essentially quantitative treatment of the data. A different approach, perhaps based on case studies of specific types of social worker-volunteer collaboration, might have allowed for the quality of their relationships to be explored more deeply. By such means it might also have been possible to study the relevance of such questions as the nature of the satisfactions that social workers expect to derive from their work; their capacity to share some of these satisfactions, and the level and quality of their training.

To investigate such matters, however, would require further research, both of a fact-finding and of a developmental nature. Nevertheless, while the depth and quality that might have been obtained through a different approach have been lost, the larger number of social workers concerned in this survey has provided a more adequate basis for generalisation. Moreover, in so far as the statistical analysis suggests meaningful relationships between some of the variables considered, the inquiry has generated some hypotheses for further testing.

NOTES

1 Northern Ireland had to be excluded owing to the difficulties of time and cost involved in making the necessary initial approach and subsequent follow-up before distributing the questionnaires.

2 These were defined as follows:
   (a) area-based staff—i.e. area officers or their equivalents; deputy/assistant area officers; senior social workers; other social workers; trainee social workers. Social work assistants were also included, although not strictly members of the profession, since the pilot results had shown them as carrying substantial case-loads and being likely to use volunteers;
   (b) centrally-based staff, only if they carried a caseload.

3 Twenty-four sample authorities were selected by using the estimates of social work staff in each local authority in Great Britain, made available to us by the Statistics Branch of the DHSS and the Scottish and Welsh offices respectively. Local authorities were first grouped into: English counties by region; Welsh counties; Scottish regions; metropolitan districts by region; inner London boroughs and outer London boroughs. Within each group, local authorities were then placed in descending order of the percentage of the total social worker population who were trainees and social work or welfare assistants. A systematic selection was then made of one in five local authorities, this giving: eight counties; two regions; seven metropolitan districts; four outer London boroughs and two inner London boroughs.

4 In all, the sample of local authority social workers approached exceeded the original estimate by over one hundred; and the total sample (in spite of a proportionately smaller selection rate for the probation officers) exceeded it by nearly 350.

5 One of these supplementary questionnaires asked for information concerning the incidence, scale and scope of volunteer use by social work staff in the office as a whole; the employment or otherwise of a volunteer organiser or other delegated person; and the types of procedure, if any, for the selection, training and supervision of volunteers. The second questionnaire related to different aspects of the work setting and asked for information concerning the number and types of referrals and allocations of the previous month; the allocation procedures and the types of team organisation; the number of social work staff, including outstanding vacancies; and the ratio of qualified to unqualified staff.

6 These exclude questionnaires returned but subsequently found to be unproductive or invalid in some way.

7 Similar differences in the response rates of probation and local authority staff (75 per cent and 52 per cent respectively) were found in the survey carried out by the Office of Manpower Economics for the Butterworth Committee (1972). In this survey, a response rate of 64 per cent was achieved from a smaller sample than that in the present inquiry.

8 Since the response rate from area offices was only just over 50 per cent, the supplementary data obtained from the two additional questionnaires do not relate to the full sample of respondents, but to just under three-quarters of them. This smaller sample however, when tested for its representativeness, corresponded to the main sample in all the relevant characteristics tested, such as designation, age, sex, social work qualifications and the use of volunteers. Area offices from which supplementary information was obtained were also compared with those of the main sample for their geographical distribution. The analysis showed that only in respect of the questionnaire relating to the work setting were the returns slightly biased in favour of metropolitan district area offices.

PART ONE   THE SOCIAL WORKERS

2 The Profession Described

INTRODUCTION

One result of the present inquiry is that the social worker population employed in the statutory services of Great Britain can now be described much more fully than hitherto. The information obtained not only shows its age, sex and job structure but also throws light on the professional qualifications and experience of social workers. It gives a picture also of the extent to which the social work profession represents a 'second' career, open to individuals of varied backgrounds and age groups. In addition to its intrinsic interest, the new data presented in this chapter provide an essential introduction to the main research findings. Moreover, it has been possible to examine each of the attributes described here for its possible relevance to the use of volunteers.

THE LOCAL AUTHORITY SAMPLE

The reorganisation of the social services in the early 1970s established a new hierarchical structure of management and control in social work, and new career possibilities for social workers. These changes allowed for more careers in the management and administration of social work, as distinct from its practice. Indeed, over recent years there has been considerable debate as to whether, in the interests of their careers, social workers are sometimes forced to choose between an administrative and a professional role, and as to how far the management function in social work is in conflict with professional needs.

The numerical balance in 1974 between management and other status levels in the structure of the newly organised services was shown by Table 1.1 in Chapter 1. At that time, management and supervisory posts apparently accounted for one in five of all social worker posts in the local authority social services departments of Great Britain, and one in four, if social work assistants and trainees are excluded. For every management and supervisory post, therefore, there were three fieldworkers, and for every fieldworker a fractional part of a social work assistant.

There is a similar pattern in the present inquiry. Management and supervisory posts are somewhat over-represented in the sample because of the slightly higher response from these groups to the inquiry. Moreover, the senior posts in the sample do not include personnel from central social services departments. Distinguishing senior social workers from area officers and their deputies, however, it seems that for every management position in the present sample, there are almost two senior social workers, and for every senior, almost four fieldworkers (Figure 2.1).

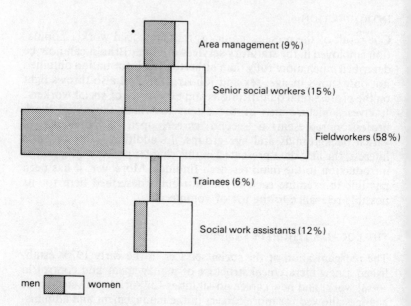

Area management (9%)

Senior social workers (15%)

Fieldworkers (58%)

Trainees (6%)

Social work assistants (12%)

men ▢ women

Figure 2.1   *The social worker hierarchy in local authority services.*
   Source: Table: 1.1.

Gender and Age

Superimposed on this hierarchical structure of social work are the sex and age distributions of social workers. First, though it is still a predominantly female profession, with women outnumbering men in the ratio of three to two, the situation is entirely reversed in the senior and management positions. Almost seven in ten of all area management posts and nearly as many senior posts are occupied by men. In comparison, men occupy only just over one in three of all fieldworker posts and fewer than one in five of all social work assistant posts.[1]

This tendency towards a disproportionate representation of men in the higher levels of the staff structure is well known and has been observed in other studies (e.g. Neill *et al.*, 1973; Jenkins and Aldridge, 1975). The explanation for it is apparently not associated with the fact that men are older on average than women, or more experienced in social work. Proportionately, rather more of them, however, are qualified. The latter may be one factor underlying the disproportion.[2] There is also the suggestion of Jenkins and Aldridge that this tendency may be due not so much to discrimination in favour of men as to the reluctance of women to seek promotion to management and administrative posts, sometimes because they prefer to remain in fieldwork. Whatever the reasons, the result, as the findings of the present inquiry confirm, is a general movement of men into the management of social work.

Secondly, the data on the age composition of the social worker sample support the view that the social work profession, like that of teachers, is largely staffed by the relatively young.[3] Nearly one-half of the social workers in the present inquiry are under the age of 35 and the great majority are under the age of 45. The average age of the sample as a whole is just under 38 years (Table 2.1).

Table 2.1   *Present age according to designation:*
local authority social workers

Present age (years)	Area officers/ deputies	Senior social workers	Field workers	Trainees	Hospital-based social workers	Social work assistants	Total
			(% of total)				
Under 25	—	2	15	45	11	15	13
25–34	25	46	39	32	26	17	34
35–44	35	22	19	15	17	30	22
45–54	27	21	19	6	31	30	22
Over 54	11	8	7	2	14	5	8
No reply	1	1	1	—	1	3	1
TOTAL[1]	100	100	100	100	100	100	100
(number)	(96)	(160)	(610)	(65)	(168)	(121)	(1,220)
Average age (*years*)	42.4	38.6	36.7	29.9	41.0	39.5	37.9

[1] Including no replies.

There are, however, differences in age composition according to designation. Area management and social work assistants, for example, contain smaller proportions of the under-35s compared with seniors, fieldworkers, and in particular trainees.

The differences are naturally reflected in the average age for each designation, which rises with seniority from nearly 30 years for trainees to 42 years for area management. Seniors are slightly younger, on average than social work assistants (38½ years and 39½ years respectively) while fieldworkers are slightly younger still (36½ years).

Full-time and Part-time Employment

Since the social work profession is staffed predominantly by women, it was to be expected that the sample would contain part-time workers. This indeed was so, but not on any large scale. Only one in eight of the local authority sample were working part-time and virtually all of these were women, mostly field-workers over the age of 35. This is a considerably lower rate than for the employed female population as a whole (Department of Employment, 1976). A considerably higher proportion of hospital-based social workers are part-time, however, perhaps because this group contains first, a much higher-than-average proportion of women and secondly, the highest proportion of those aged 45 and over. There may also be a further explanation. In the days before the integration of medical social workers and psychiatric social workers into the local authority services, more women seeking part-time social work may have been attracted into the hospital field, since it is said that 'more imaginative use' was made of them in the National Health Service than by local authorities (Andrews, 1974). The changeover following the National Health Service Reorganisation Act of 1973 occurred in 1974, and it is unlikely, therefore, that there would have been many changes in policy or practice affecting part-time social workers based in hospitals by the time of this inquiry.

Length of Experience in Social Work

In view of the public references that are made from time to time about the relative inexperience of many social workers today, it is important to note that their average period of experience amounts to just over seven and a half years.[4] Nearly a quarter of the sample had been in social work for ten years or more, though there was an equivalent number with less than two years, presumably reflecting the recent expansion of the service.

There were, however, as was to be expected, considerable variations in social work experience according to designation and age, the years spent in social work rising both with increasing seniority and with age. Thus, the average length of experience of area officers (15.4 years) far exceeded that of fieldworkers (6.7 years) which, in turn, was longer than that of social work assistants, though only by just over two and a half years.

There were marked differences also in the length of social work experience between the age groups, indicating that entry to the social work profession has been available to a wide age range, and that the average age at entry, which for the sample as a whole is at about 30, may have fallen in recent years (Table 2.2).[5]

Table 2.2   *Estimated average age of entry to social work according to present age: local authority social workers*

| | Present age | | | | | |
	Under 25	25-34	35-44	45-54	Over 54	Total
			(years)			
Average length of experience in social work	2.3	5.1	5.7	10.2	17.3	7.7
Average present age	22.5	30.0	40.0	50.0	58.5	37.9
Estimated age, on average, at entry to social work	20.2	24.9	34.3	39.8	41.2	30.2
TOTAL number	(160)	(419)	(263)	(265)	(97)	(1,204)

Length of Time in Present Post

The average stay of social workers in their present posts was only just over three years. This reflects, perhaps, the changes in recent years in both local government boundaries and functions, and the rise in employment of social workers by local authority social services departments. A substantial proportion of the sample had, moreover, been in their present posts with their present authorities for less than one year, and over one-half for less than two years.

These proportions were in part due to the comparatively short periods of service of the younger social workers in the sample, particularly the under-25s. Indeed, as would be expected, averages for length of time in the present post rose steadily with age from just over one year for the youngest, to over eight years for the oldest age groups, among whom a relatively large proportion had been in their present posts for over ten years.

Differences were less marked for designation than for age groups. Social workers in management positions, for example, had on average occupied their present posts for only a little longer than fieldworkers. Sharper differences between the designations emerged, however, when the average length of time spent in each type of post was expressed as a percentage of the average years of social work experience for each designation. This showed that, while average years spent in social work and time spent in their present posts were greater for those in management and senior positions than for others, their present posts represented a smaller part of their total work experience. Thus for area officers the experience represented by their present jobs was just over one-quarter of their total social work experience, whereas for fieldworkers, as Table 2.3 shows, the present post represented almost one-half of their total social work experience.

Table 2.3 *Proportion of total experience in social work represented by time in present post according to designation: local authority social workers*

	Area officers/ deputies	Senior social workers	Field workers	Train- ees	Hos- pital- based social workers	Social work assis- tants	Total
				(years)			
Average length of experience in social work	15·4	10·3	6·7	2·0	10·3	4·0	7·5
Average length of time in present post	4·0	3·3	3·1	1·1	4·8	3·2	3·3
				(%)			
Proportion of total social work experience represented by time in present post	26	32	46	55	47	80	44
TOTAL number	(96)	(160)	(610)	(65)	(168)	(121)	(1,220)

One interpretation of these differences is that job changes are more frequent in the higher than in the lower ranks of the social services career structure, these figures, as might be expected, partly reflecting the movement of the more experienced social workers into the more senior posts.

Qualifications
Social work qualifications are a subject of argument and debate. There is the call to increase the numbers of recruits for training so as to achieve, within as short a time as possible, a fully qualified profession. This view is advocated by BASW and is supported by many practitioners, managers and teachers in the profession. On the other hand, it has been argued that the present complement of qualified social workers is used inefficiently and that higher levels of social work output could be achieved, for any given level of

Table 2.4   *Primary qualifications of social workers*

Primary qualifications	Local authority social workers	Probation officers
Social work qualifications	*(% of total)*	
Certificate in Social Work (CSW) of the CTSW	11	4
Certificate of Qualification (CQSW) of the CCETSW	16	9
specialist certificate in		
child care	7	1
other[1]	11	71
sub-total	45	85
Related qualifications[2]	9	–
Other qualifications		
degrees, diplomas in social studies and other degrees	14	2
other (including nursing)	15	1
In training	5	10
None of the above	9	1
No reply	3	1
TOTAL[3]	100[4]	100
(number)	(1,099)	(191)

[1] Including probation work/medical social work/psychiatric social work/ family casework.

[2] Including certificates for work with the deaf or blind and for recognition of experience.

[3] Excluding social work assistants.

[4] Excluding ancillaries.

expenditure, by greater use of ancillary workers (Judge, 1977).

Despite appearances, these two arguments do not necessarily conflict, since there is no *a priori* reason why a fully qualified profession cannot be assisted by ancillary workers. It is well known, however, that the majority of social workers practising in local authorities today are unqualified. Our findings confirm this. On the basis of primary qualifications in social work, just under one-half of the men and just over one-third of the women were qualified at the time of the inquiry (Table 2.4).[6] If, however, as seems likely, the employment of social work assistants by social services departments is growing, and if, as Bamford (1977) suggests, volunteers are increasingly regarded by the statutory services as ancillary workers, then, other things being equal, the unqualified may constitute an even higher proportion of personnel based in local authorities and involved in the practice of social work. Under such conditions, the respective functions of the qualified and the unqualified may be even more sharply differentiated than is suggested by our evidence (see Chapters 9 and 10). The qualified may, perhaps, become increasingly specialised and further away from the generic model if, as Barr (1973) suggests, they are 'cast in the role of technical consultant', the emphasis being on 'the development of new diagnostic skills, and away from face-to-face contact with clients'. It is the view of many practising social workers, however, that specialisation does not necessarily imply the ending of caseloads. They refer to the structure of medical care—a frequent point of reference for social workers—where the medical consultant is still working directly with patients.

The idea of an 'adjunctive role' in which the professionally qualified social worker would play his or her part through the medium of advice and co-ordination persists, and is underlined in the BASW Report (1977). Indeed the Report concludes that to have one qualified worker for each client is not an appropriate model for the most effective use of fieldwork personnel, and questions whether all fieldworkers' jobs qualify as social work in the Working Party's meaning of the activity. Naturally, if social work is redefined so that, by and large, only those at present qualified may be assumed to be practising it, its professional standing would be somewhat higher than is the case at the moment.

For those who are qualified, the type of qualification held is clearly influenced by what has been available to social work candidates at different times. Up to 1972, for example, it was possible to qualify only in the main branches of social work so that social workers qualifying before that time necessarily hold some form of 'specialist' certificate. In 1972, however, the Central Council for Education and Training in Social Work (CCETSW) validated a wide range of courses, and thereafter issued the Certificate of Qualification in Social Work (CQSW). There is also, at the time of writing, the Certificate in Residential Social Work (CRSW).

These changes are reflected in the variations in primary social work qualifications in the local authority sample according to age as well as to designation. The younger social workers are more likely to have acquired the CQSW, whereas the older social workers are more frequently qualified in child care, medical social work, psychiatric social work and the like. As Table 2.5 shows, management staff, too, are much more likely to hold such qualifications—those of child care predominating—whereas most fieldworkers hold the CQSW.

The proportion of qualified staff also varies according to age and designation, the most qualified being those aged 25-44, and management and senior staff. Among younger social workers fewer, proportionately, have social work qualifications and

Table 2.5 *Primary qualifications according to designation: local authority social workers*

Primary qualifications	Area officers/ deputies	Senior social workers	Field workers	Trainees	Hospital-based social workers
			(% of total)		
Social work qualifications					
Certificate in Social Work (CSW) of the CTSW	23	22	9	—	3
Certificate of Qualification (CQSW) of the CCETSW	2	19	20	—	10
Specialist certificate in					
Child Care	31	17	3	2	2
other[1]	18	11	5	—	32
sub-total	74	69	37	2	47
Related and other qualifications[2]	21	27	45	60	35
In training	3	3	4	20	4
None of the above	2	1	10	17	13
No reply	—	—	4	1	1
TOTAL[3]	100	100	100	100	100
(number)	(96)	(160)	(610)	(65)	(168)

[1] Including probation work/medical social work/psychiatric social work/ family casework.

[2] Including certificates for work with the deaf or blind and for recognition of experience; degrees, diplomas in social studies and other degrees; and other (including nursing).

[3] Excluding social work assistants.

more hold academic degrees. This is presumably linked with the fact that many of those with degrees may expect to gain their social work qualifications through secondment at a later stage. Current financial cutbacks may prejudice the fulfilment of these expectations. The most recent recruits to social work also tend to be less often qualified irrespective of age. Thus even excluding social work assistants and trainees, recruitment in recent years, as in the early post-war years, has been greater among unqualified than qualified staff.

Previous Employment
As mentioned earlier, entry to social work occurs over a wide age span. It also attracts recruits from a variety of work backgrounds. In the present inquiry, the majority (two in three) of social workers had had previous jobs or careers, leaving these at some stage in their lives to take up social work.[7]

The incidence of previous employment varied, however, being

highest among area management and social work assistants, and lowest amongst those who were hospital-based. Proportionately more men than women had had previous work experience, and the incidence was markedly higher after the age of 25. For most social workers over this age, therefore, social work was their second career at least, and not that which they had first chosen or entered.

The former jobs of social workers were distributed over an extensive range of occupations, including unskilled manual work and the higher professions. Proportionately more social workers came into social work from the intermediate professional, managerial and technical occupations (like teaching, nursing, social welfare, central and local government, management) than from occupations in the lower socio-economic groups—both non-manual and manual.

Proportionately more men than women, however, had come into social work from manual occupations, while more women than men had previously worked in mainly clerical occupations. Younger social workers (the under-25s) and trainees were also more likely than others to have been previously employed in clerical occupations.

Since data on upward and downward social mobility are measured mainly in terms of occupational changes, we traced the movement that had occurred between the present and the former occupations of the social worker sample. Though the estimates can be only approximate and related to the movement between combinations of socio-economic groups, the results indicate that over one in four of the sample (excluding the social work assistants) raised their socio-economic level, if not their social class, by leaving their former employment and entering social work.[8] This suggests that social work is one of the intermediate positions in the social stratification system of industrial society which, as Goldthorpe (1967) has argued, widens the movement upward from the lower levels, providing a second chance for individuals who, for one reason or another, started their working lives lower down the social scale.

School-leaving Age
It is well established that social class factors influence the age of leaving school, and thus the levels of occupational achievement, even among children of equal measured ability. It seemed of interest to discover the school-leaving background of the social work profession in the hope that, in the absence of data concerning parental occupations, this information would give an indication, albeit a rough and ready one, of the social class composition of the sample.

The majority of respondents had left school at the age of seventeen years or later. Just under one in five had ended their school days at the age of fifteen, or earlier, and virtually an equal number at the age of sixteen.

There were, however, some variations in this general pattern according to sex, designation and age. Proportionately twice as many men as women for example, had left school at the age of fifteen or before. Early leaving also tended to be more frequent among the social work assistants, but far less so among trainees and hospital-based social workers. The most striking differences, however, were between the different age groups, the proportion of leavers at the age of fifteen or before, and at sixteen, rising slightly after the age of 25, but steeply after the age of 35. This contrast in the length of secondary school life between the under-35s and the over-35s suggests that the social basis of recruitment, and hence the social composition of the social work profession, may be undergoing some change.

A further indication of this was evident when the estimated social class origins of different age groups in the same were compared.[9] The social class pattern differed as between the younger and the older social workers. The under-35s were more frequently drawn from families of non-manual workers in the professional, administrative and intermediate occupations than from families of manual workers.

This shift in the ratio of manual to non-manual family backgrounds would be consistent with the trend already noted towards a longer school life among the younger social workers. It is possible, therefore, that the social basis of recruitment to social work may be changing. More precise information would be required to verify the extent and nature of any such change.

Membership of a Professional Association
Since 1970, the two main professional associations for social workers have been BASW and the National Association of Probation Officers (NAPO). Only a minority of local authority social workers in the survey, however, belonged to BASW, and the great majority to neither association. (There is, as will be seen, a proportionately much higher incidence of professional affiliation in the probation sample.) It might seem that these membership figures reflect the numerous unqualified social workers in the social services, to whom full membership of BASW is closed.[10] But this would not explain the fact that BASW membership is not very high even among the qualified, the proportions falling steadily from the more senior to the basic-grade qualified workers, and from the older to the younger.

These findings raise doubts as to how far social work may claim to be a profession, if the great majority of those who practise it and earn their living by doing so are not members of the association which speaks for the profession and seeks to establish and maintain professional standards. In the future, however, it may be the registration of social workers rather than their BASW membership which would give them the claim to professional status.[11]

THE PROBATION SAMPLE

The probation officers, as Table 2.6 shows, present a rather different picture in almost every respect examined from that described for the local authority social workers.

Table 2.6   *Characteristics of probation officers*

Characteristic	*Probation officers (% of total)*
Designation	
Senior probation officers	27
Probation officers	67
Ancillary workers	4
Other	2
Age (years)	
Under 25	3
25-34	26
35-44	28
45-54	31
55 and over	11
No reply	1
TOTAL	100
(number)	(203)
	(years)
Average age	41·6
Average length of experience in social work	9.9
Average length of time with present authority	4·8

Thus, men outnumber women in the probation service in the same ratio as women outnumber men in the local authority service—three to two. The age distribution of probation officers is also different. There are rather higher proportions in the over-45 age group, compared with local authority social workers, so that their average age of 41.6 years is higher. Proportionately more of the probation officers are in senior positions; also their average experience in social work and time in their present posts are a little longer compared with local authority social workers. A much higher proportion of them entered the probation service from other types of employment, though there were few differences between the two samples concerning the types of employment previously followed. A much higher proportion of them (almost twice as many as of local authority social workers) were qualified, their qualifications being mainly in probation work as is consistent with a specialised service. Finally, the great majority are members of their professional association.

THE USE OF VOLUNTEERS

At the outset of the study, we assumed that certain personal characteristics and attributes of social workers might influence the extent to which they are involved with volunteers, the ways in which they use their services and their attitudes towards them. In the event, this assumption was not confirmed. Apart from a few marginal differences in attitudes and some very slight variations in the incidence of volunteer use, only one of the many personal factors examined—job status—seems directly relevant to the use of volunteers by social workers, and then mainly, as will be seen, because of the links between this and caseload size and composition.

Even their own experiences of volunteering in the social work field has, it seems, no appreciable influence on the professionals' later practices regarding volunteers. It might be supposed that people who had themselves been volunteers would, in their professional capacity, be more inclined than others to use the services of volunteers. But our findings did not bear this out. Just under one-half of the local authority social workers (marginally fewer men, proportionately, than women) had had experience of voluntary work themselves. Such experience seems to have been relatively more frequent amongst the youngest workers than among any of the older, and this may perhaps reflect the increasing provision in recent years of opportunities for young volunteers by schools, youth organisations, community service agencies and the like. Yet, when former volunteers come to be salaried social workers themselves, they are no more than marginally disposed to use the services of volunteers to a greater extent than their fellows. Nor do their attitudes towards volunteers, or assessments of their use, show any sign of being influenced by their own past experiences.

The finding that the personal attributes of social workers themselves appear not to have direct bearing on their use of volunteers is an important outcome of the present inquiry. It applies equally to the probation sample. It suggests, as will be seen, that variations in the incidence and scale of volunteer use are to be explained, not by individual differences between one social worker and another, but by differences in the work they do.

SUMMARY

Social workers in local authority social services are predominantly women—except in management and senior posts, where men are by far the majority—and are mainly in basic-grade posts. There are sizeable proportions of management and senior staff at the higher levels, and of social work assistants at the lower levels, of what is clearly a hierarchical staff structure. They are relatively young, with an average age of just under 38 years and with an average length of social work experience of just over seven years. Their entry to the profession is on average at the age of 30. Fewer than one-half have any social work qualifications and only a small minority are members of a professional association. Most of them have taken up social work from other types of employment, a move which, in about one in four instances, seems to have improved their socio-economic status. There are indications that the average age of entering social work has fallen in recent years, that the social composition of the profession may be changing, and that an increasing proportion of new recruits are unqualified. Only job status of the many personal factors examined seems directly relevant to the use of volunteers.

Probation officers are mainly men, with a slightly higher average age than that of the local authority social workers and longer work experience. More of them, proportionately, entered social work from other types of employment, have the relevant qualifications and are members of their professional association.

NOTES

1 The same tendency applied to hospital-based social workers where the proportion of men employed is even lower than for those based in area offices.
2 The age group containing the highest proportion of men in the BASW membership survey (28-32) roughly corresponds to the 25-34 group in the present inquiry, which showed a similar pattern. It is possible that an explanation for the higher representation of men in this age group may have something to do with the age at which they first entered social work. If, as estimated later, the average age of entry of the 25-34 group was about 25, this may have been the age when many women withdrew from professional work because of family responsibilities. Further analysis of the data would, however, be required in order to verify this.
3 The two professions were compared with the occupational and socio-economic group to which they belong in the Census classification, Great Britain Census, 1971).
4 Length of experience included any time spent as a social work assistant or

trainee, as well as part-time employment in social work. It excluded voluntary social work.

5 By subtracting the average length of experience in social work for each age group from the equivalent average age, an approximate age of entry to social work may be calculated. Since the age of entry to social work is substantially higher for those in the older age groups than in the younger, social workers may now be entering the profession at a younger age than was the case in previous years. This would seem to be confirmed by the large proportion of under-35s relative to older age groups in the sample of social workers.

6 In the analysis, a primary qualification was allotted to each social worker, specialist taking precedence over general certificates, and social work qualification over other kinds.

7 For the purposes of analysis, occupations were grouped according to the socio-economic categories and occupation orders shown in the *Classification of Occupations*, HMSO, 1960. Difficulties arose in classifying occupations which were not fully described, or for which the descriptions were too general, e.g. 'engineering', 'farming'. Where there was uncertainty, occupations were classified as 'inadequately described'. These are not included in the general analysis. Also excluded from the classification were temporary occupations and vacation work or casual types of employment.

8 Social work assistants were excluded from this analysis since the classification of their occupation as equivalent to the socio-economic level of social workers is in some doubt.

9 On the assumption that the association between age of leaving school and father's occupation was not very different for social workers than for the population at large, estimates were made of the proportions in each school-leaving group likely to fall within one of six social class categories. These estimates were based on the proportion in each age-of-leaving group falling within social class groups I, II, III (non-manual), III (manual), IV and V, in a sample inquiry carried out by the Government Social Survey in 1966 (Schools Council, 1966). This survey was based on a population of 4,618 pupils aged 13-16 in 150 maintained secondary schools.

10 This was, at the time of the inquiry, and is at the time of writing, a matter of controversy among BASW members and beyond. Associate membership is offered to those without qualifications, and indeed a very few of our respondents specified this type of membership. They are included in the figures as members but their numbers make virtually no difference to the totals.

11 See *The Times*, 19 July 1977.

3 A View of Themselves

INTRODUCTION

In planning the present inquiry, and with the postal method of collecting data particularly in mind, we thought it essential in our questionnaire to give social workers a chance to comment freely on some issues of close concern to them. Of these, their hopes and aspirations for their careers, and their satisfactions or frustrations about their work, had already been discussed in some depth during the exploratory phase of the study. We felt they were relevant not only to the use of volunteers but also to an understanding of the present feelings and attitudes of social workers.

Within the scope of the present inquiry, it was not possible to do more than touch lightly on all these questions. We tried, however, to cover the more important of them—their early hopes, the satisfactions or otherwise of working with clients, and their views on their own effectiveness.

EARLY HOPES

While we could not attempt any systematic probing of social workers' reasons for taking up social work, we nevertheless thought it would be interesting to try to discover something about their hopes and aspirations concerning the choices they had made. Two in three of the sample had entered social work from some other type of employment, so that it was their second career at least and a chance for some to raise their socio-economic status.

In devising suitable questions, Pearson's study (1973) of social work recruits seemed particularly relevant. Pearson chose social work recruits for examining motivations for entering social work because, since they had not yet participated in the professional culture, he considered they were less likely to have imbibed the kind of conventional, sentimental and theoretical constructs of motivation which, in his view, often characterised the more established social workers' accounts and explanations of their actions. He accordingly asked a sample of seventy-three social work students of both sexes (mostly in their twenties) to complete two statements. The first indicated what, through entering social work, they hoped to achieve—the second, what they hoped to avoid. We decided to use these two questions in the present inquiry.

What Social Workers Hoped to Achieve

In a general sense, the findings of the present inquiry for the local authority and the probation services confirm Pearson's theory that the choice of social work as an occupation represents for the individuals concerned an attempt to find a way by which they may more easily experience themselves as human beings. As Table 3.1 shows, most practising social workers, as well as new recruits to the profession, evidently hope to find in social work some form of self-realisation, and reject in many cases other types of work or occupation which do not offer this.

Table 3.1   *What respondents hoped to achieve by coming into social work*

What hoped to achieve	Local authority social workers (% of total)	Probation officers
Having a satisfying/useful job	40	32
Helping people, being of value	34	41
Effecting changes in client and client's situation, community/society	17	10
Achieving happiness and self-realisation	14	19
Gaining greater knowledge/understanding	9	5
Working with people	7	9
Other (including job security, providing a professional service)	9	13
Nothing/not very much/not sure	6	4
No reply	5	5
TOTAL[1]	100	100
(number)	(1,220)	(203)

[1] Multiple replies.

As social workers recalled their original motivations (and hardly any did not), some expressed their hopes of self-realisation quite directly. In most of the comments, however, this hope was implicit rather than explicit and took different forms. Some emphasised their hope of a satisfying and useful job; others their wish to 'give' or to help people; others hoped to acquire greater knowledge and understanding; and some to effect some kind of change. There were also some replies which combined more than one type of objective. Even so, a satisfying job and giving help to people were by far the most frequent replies, though their relative order was slightly different as between local authority social workers and probation officers.

Thus, the largest single group of local authority social workers, but not of probation officers, hoped to find in social work a satisfying, worthwhile job, and referred to their earlier hopes of achieving a 'rewarding career', 'job satisfaction in a worthwhile occupation', or 'an interesting, rewarding job with freedom, excitement and drama'. The frequent recurrence of the term, 'worthwhile' seems indicative of the hope that self-realisation would arise from the intrinsic nature of social work.

The older social workers were apparently the least often interested at the outset of their careers in achieving a satisfying job. Area management staff, particularly if qualified, were the most often so.

One-third of the local authority social workers, but rather more of the probation service, referred to their hopes of wanting to give something, or to help people in some way. Self-fulfilment, it was believed, particularly by respondents in the probation service, would come from contributing something of value for others. Sometimes this giving was seen as an end in itself, the respondents concerned wanting only to make 'a contribution to society'. More often, the hope was expressed in terms of 'getting a better deal for people'; 'an interesting career in helping others'; or simply of achieving 'a feeling of being useful'; or, as for some social workers, of just 'helping people to help themselves'.

Fewer social workers in both samples referred to their hopes of effecting some kind of change. This was related either to clients, such as 'changing unfavourable client situations', or helping clients to achieve 'a better emotional balance'; or—particularly by the under-25s—to wider social changes brought about by community or social action. One social worker had hoped to be 'participating in meaningful social change within the social fabric', and another, 'to get to know the system with a view to changing it for the better'.

Almost as many local authority social workers, but proportionately many more probation officers, were quite specific about their hopes of achieving 'self-fulfilment' and 'happiness'. Rather smaller proportions in each sample saw social work as a means of gaining greater knowledge and understanding—of acquiring 'a broader outlook', of increasing their 'self-awareness', or as a 'continued learning experience'; and fewer still saw social work as an opportunity to 'work with people' or, as in some isolated cases, to relieve or assuage what they described as their 'guilt feelings'.

What Social Workers Hoped to Avoid

Social workers evidently found it much easier to recall what they had originally hoped to achieve when choosing social work as their career, than what they had hoped to avoid, two in five (particularly the older social workers) having no comment other than 'nothing'

(Table 3.2). Among those who replied, however, the main emphasis by far was on the wish to avoid boredom in their work, though a sizeable minority also referred to their wish to avoid an 'empty' or a 'wasted' life. There is very little difference in any of these respects between the local authority and probation samples.

Table 3.2 *What respondents hoped to avoid by coming into social work*

What hoped to avoid	Local authority social workers	Probation officers
	(% of total)	
Unsatisfying work, boring/routine jobs, the rat race, etc.	67	58
Wasting their lives, stagnating, etc.	20	20
Values/ethos of materialism, industry and commerce	10	14
Other (including a specified job, insecurity, low pay)	25	21
TOTAL[1] [2]	100	100
(number)	(585)	(108)

[1] Excluding those for whom there was nothing they wished to avoid.
[2] Multiple replies.

When the emphasis was on work, it was most often that of a 'boring, routine' kind that was to be avoided. Over two-thirds of the local authority social workers who replied and nearly three-fifths of the probation officers had, in retrospect, rejected this kind of employment. For them it was the 'tedium, the repetition, the limited mechanical routine' or, as other social workers put it, 'the rat race', echoing the large proportion of Pearson's recruits who had hoped to avoid this or its equivalent by entering social work. Some respondents may indeed have escaped from such employment, given the substantial proportion of the sample who entered social work from other jobs.

Next in order of frequency were the replies of respondents who recalled, in more general terms, their hopes of avoiding a life with 'lack of purpose', giving no opportunity for 'personal development' or for using their skills and capacities. Others seem to have hoped that by coming into social work they would avoid the development of 'self-centredness and alienation' or 'a continuing hedonism'. Others had feared isolation from people or from 'reality', or 'a lifetime of no intellectual stimulus'.

A smaller group had entered the social work profession in order to avoid what they felt were 'materialistic values', or what one social worker, who had worked in industry, described as the 'striving towards long-term objectives' which he did not value. Finally, an even smaller proportion of social workers had wished to avoid a variety of things. Prominent amongst these were references to specific types of job and low pay and insecurity.

It looks as if, with the passing of time, professional indoctrination and practical experience may also influence social workers' views of their past hopes and actions. First, only half as many of the over-34s as of the under-34s referred to their wish to avoid the 'ethos of materialism' or the values of 'the competitive system'. Secondly, only a quarter as many of the over-54s as of the under-25s wished to avoid unsatisfying work. There is, in fact, a proportionately steady decline with increasing age in the incidence of references to the wish to avoid unsatisfying features of work. This suggests that the further away from the start of a career, the less likely in retrospect may social workers feel that they had wanted to avoid the 'rat race' or its equivalent, or indeed many other aspects of alternative employment. Earlier-held opinions may be forgotten, or undergo some change in a retrospective account of things. There is also the possibility that the actual work experience (if any) of the older age groups prior to entering social work, and their attitudes towards it, differed from those of the younger age groups.

REWARDS AND DRAWBACKS

Exploratory discussions with social workers during the preparatory stages of the present inquiry had shown that working with clients had special meaning for the professionals concerned, in terms of the satisfactions and disappointments that arose from this kind of work. These were clearly related to the interpersonal nature of casework, whether with individuals or groups, and to the helping process to which social workers were heavily committed.

While the subtleties and complexities of worker-client relationships could not be pursued through a postal questionnaire, we thought it important, nevertheless, to question social workers who carried caseloads on what they felt were the most rewarding aspects of working with clients at the present time and, in addition, on what they felt to be the drawbacks.[1] No direct link between their views and the use of volunteers was assumed. Nevertheless, we believed that the replies to these two questions, in revealing something of the nature of casework satisfactions and dissatisfactions, might prove relevant to the hesitation that most social workers tend to have about the intervention of volunteers in many types of casework situation.

Each question was open-ended, so as to give respondents the opportunity to comment as freely as they wished. The results indicate that casework brings a variety of satisfactions, each one with its own meaning for the social workers concerned.

The Most Rewarding Aspects

The Local Authority Sample. As was to be expected, most replies were directly client-related, though different elements of the rewards were stressed. First in order of frequency were the rewards associated with the achievement of casework objectives. Given that these, as generally accepted, are directed towards helping clients to surmount their difficulties in such a way that they are less at the mercy of inner or external forces, so over one in three of the local authority sample, and proportionately rather more of the qualified, felt their rewards came from their having witnessed, participated in, or brought about, some change for the better in their clients' situation (Table 3.3).

Table 3.3   *Most rewarding aspects of working with clients*

Most rewarding aspect	*Local authority social workers*	*Probation officers*
	(% of total)	
Client-related rewards		
change in client	20	26
relief of distress	17	8
relationships with clients	16	20
type of client group	14	5
Other rewards		
support of others	19	13
social work methods	7	10
use of skills/learning	3	3
other (including continued client contact)	7	14
None	9	8
No reply	7	9
TOTAL[1] [2]	100	100
(number)	(1,056)	(191)

[1] Caseload holders only.
[2] Multiple replies.

Opinions were fairly evenly divided, however, as to the nature of the change. One in five social workers thought it had something to do with the attitudes of clients and with their capacity to deal with their problems—some change in the 'inner' autonomy of the individual. Typical of such changes were the rewards that came from 'helping a client gain insight', 'seeing families with what seemed insurmountable problems now coping', and 'the calming down of adolescents who were very difficult in the past'. Nearly as many social workers, however, particularly those with the larger caseloads, the unqualified social workers and social work assistants, felt that the change for the better had been because of the actual relief of distress or improvement in the external conditions of their clients.

A second important source of satisfaction related to social workers' feelings about their clients, and the respect for and concern about them that had developed over the course of time. One social worker referred to the 'continual reaffirmation of people's qualities and potential and their resilience in spite of what we professionals try to do'.

Thirdly, there were those who emphasised the rewarding nature of working with particular client groups or types of problem. In some instances, this reflected the particular satisfactions derived from following more specialised interests, using more specialised skills and carrying out more intensive casework.

Underlying the rewarding nature of each of these client-related elements was undoubtedly the satisfaction—perhaps the prime one—of feeling useful and valued. References were made, for example, not only to the clients' responses to the social workers' professional skills, but to their appreciation of what the social workers themselves were trying to do. Thus, the rewards for one social worker were that on leaving a client, doubtful as to what had been achieved, she returned to find, not only changes in the situation, but that these were attributed to the social worker's intervention. In so far as this intervention was successful, appreciated and combined with the expressed wish on the client's part for it to continue, so it helped to reaffirm and enhance the social worker's feelings of being helpful and useful, and to sustain the original hopes of having a useful and worthwhile career. This, as we have seen, was in the minds of many when they first decided to take up social work.

A different source of satisfaction was the support and encouragement of colleagues (such comments came less frequently from social work assistants than from others). This seems relevant to the view put forward in the Lynch Inquiry (1976) that, for some social workers, friendship patterns among them, and co-operative relationships generally, may have a strong emotional appeal as well as being functional for their work.

The rewards that came mainly from using particular social work methods, including the management of resources, were referred to by relatively small minorities. Even smaller proportions commented on the satisfaction derived from using their skills, training and experience, or from the further development of these as a result of their casework experience. Relatively few social workers at the time of the inquiry felt that there were no rewards from working with clients.

It seems, however, that the longer social workers remain in social work, the less likely they are to feel that there are any rewards of this kind. Thus, those with the longest experience are not only the least likely to feel rewarded by some change in their clients, or by the support of their colleagues, they are also the least likely to feel that there are any rewards at all in working with clients.

There was also some cynicism expressed, such as the view of the senior social worker who felt she would have 'to look very hard to find a rewarding aspect at the present time'. For her, 'over-involvement and starry beliefs of the past had been eroded by stress' and by rationalising her approach to meet the lack of resources. Reward, for her, was 'closing a case'.

The rewards for some social workers had several aspects, no one of which took priority. Thus, one social worker felt that her rewards were threefold—her clients were appreciative, she was in her view effecting changes, and she was able to pursue her specialist interests. Another found that her rewards came not only from her success in changing a situation but also from having a specialised role, which allowed her to concentrate on clients in whom she was specially interested.

The Probation Sample. In the Butterworth Inquiry (1972), probation officers were found to be more satisfied, in certain respects, with their jobs than were their counterparts in social services departments. It is, therefore, of interest to note that in the present inquiry probation officers' views did not differ substantially from those of local authority staff on the nature of the rewards of working with clients. True, rather fewer probation officers commented on the satisfaction derived from relieving distress or, naturally enough perhaps in view of their more specialised work, from working with specific groups of clients. Moreover, probation officers did not comment nearly so fully, so that there were fewer multiple replies. Allowing for such differences, it would seem that generally, among both samples, the rewarding aspects of working with clients are not very different from those of the staff of the pre-Seebohm welfare and probation services who participated in the Jeffreys inquiry (1965) over fifteen years ago. The majority of those also found that the most rewarding aspect of their work was helping people in need.

The Main Drawbacks

The Local Authority Sample. Social workers were also asked for their views on what they felt at the time to be the main drawbacks of working with clients. By far the most important for almost all designations—accounting for two in five of all replies—was the scarcity of resources (Table 3.4). This scarcity was far more often referred to in a general sense—'the financial cutbacks', 'the absolute poverty of resources', and 'the lack of material help, which limits the assistance we can give'—than in a specific sense— 'the mismanagement of the resources we have', the 'shortage of residential homes', the 'lack of good places for adolescents', or the 'lack of children's homes and facilities for the mentally handi- capped'.

Table 3.4   *Main drawbacks of working with clients*

Main drawbacks	Local authority social workers	Probation officers
	(% of total)	
Resources and facilities		
general	29	12
specific	13	7
sub-total	42	19
Workload pressures		
lack of time	20	22
general	19	–
sub-total	39	22
Role conflict/uncertainties	9	5
Staff shortages/difficulties	8	3
Organisation, structure, etc.	7	4
Personal to social workers	4	5
Other	11	8
None	17	26
No reply	4	4
TOTAL[1][2]	100	100
(number)	(1,056)	(191)

[1] Caseload holders only.
[2] Multiple replies.

This emphasis on the scarcity of resources is interesting in several respects. First, it represented a major source of dissatisfaction in the Jeffreys study, where one-third of the sample commented adversely on the absence or shortage of facilities to help clients. Secondly, since in the present inquiry social workers' comments were made before the most recent series of cuts in the social services, it may be assumed that, as the situation worsens, their dissatisfactions on this score are likely to increase. Thirdly, as will be seen later, it proved to be one of the important factors in undermining the social workers' feelings of effectiveness.

Yet another scarce resource was time, some referring to the 'lack of time to look beyond people's immediate needs', to hear the 'real core of problems', to 'consider social work issues', 'to do any work in depth', or for 'studying and training'. One in five commented on the time factor, particularly the qualified senior social workers. Almost as frequent (though not for social work assistants) were references to the pressures and demands of workloads, or 'the sheer volume of work', of the 'large caseloads', of the 'skewed nature of referrals, because social services are regarded as a source of income maintenance'.

Just under one in ten of the replies contained references to difficulties that social workers felt were due to conflicts, ambiguities and confusion in their role *vis-à-vis* society at large, the general public, clients and other agencies. Such difficulties resulted, in the view of one respondent, in 'social workers becoming classed as interfering busybodies who are not sufficiently in touch with their clients'. The frequency of these references to role conflict rose steadily with seniority to almost one in five of area management staff. There was thus much greater unanimity of viewpoint on the scarcity of resources than on some of the other drawbacks mentioned.

Smaller minorities were worried by organisational and administrative factors. Some emphasised the shortcomings of bureaucracies—'the top-heavy and cumbersome administrative machine', the 'institutionalisation of "caring"', and 'bureaucratic joylessness'. Such factors as the lack of variety in their work with clients, or their own personal shortcomings, were also commented upon by respondents, though more often by the least experienced in social work. Moreover, one in six social workers (and more than one in three social work assistants) felt there were no drawbacks at all to their present work with clients—almost twice as many as those who felt that there were no rewards.

The Probation Sample. Though the rewards found by probation officers were much the same as those by local authority social workers, their dissatisfactions were of a different order. Proportionately far fewer probation staff raised the question of scarce resources, while higher proportions felt there were no drawbacks at all. The most frequent source of dissatisfaction was evidently that of insufficient time. This suggests that, while corresponding to local authority social workers in terms of their satisfactions, probation officers are less often dissatisfied with the aspects of their work discussed here. This would be consistent with the findings of other studies (Jeffreys, 1965; Butterworth, 1972).

VIEWS ON EFFECTIVENESS

Though it may be assumed that social workers' satisfactions and dissatisfactions contribute in various ways to their feelings of effectiveness, we thought it important to invite more specific references to their view of themselves. Social workers were asked, therefore, first to say what single factor they felt was the most undermining of their effectiveness as a social worker and secondly, what single factor was the most helpful.

The Most Undermining Factor
Several interesting features emerged from the replies as can be seen from Table 3.5. First, the two most frequently cited undermining factors—scarcity of resources and pressures of work—are also the two main sources of their dissatisfactions. Secondly, the source of social workers' dissatisfactions was not, in all cases, felt to be the most important adverse influence on their effectiveness. In other words, these two factors occur more often as drawbacks than as undermining factors. Thirdly, this seems to be partly due to the fact that a sizeable minority, especially among the women and among social work assistants, saw their own shortcomings—their lack of skill, experience, training or self-confidence—as being more undermining to them than any external factors. Moreover, where these feelings of inadequacy were expressed, they sometimes betokened quite serious self-doubts, reference being made to 'a lack of confidence', 'becoming too involved at moments of crisis', and 'a sense of insecurity'. Age is again an influencing factor with these self-critical attitudes, the under-25s being most affected. Fourthly, staff shortages and difficulties, and organisational weaknesses, including the shortcomings of what were described as 'top heavy', 'hierarchical' and 'bureaucratic' structures, were each rather more often cited as undermining factors (in decreasing frequency with increasing age) than as sources of dissatisfaction. In the first instance, there were references to shortages of qualified social workers, as well as clerical and administrative staff, and to the lack of supervision and poor support from seniors and management—'not just managerial oversight of the caseload', but a failure to look at 'the salient dynamics of on-going casework'. In the second instance, social workers commented on the increasing frustrations of not being able 'to make a stand or make one's own decisions', of 'too many links in the communication chain', of 'the inability of departments to delegate', or of 'those at the top' being 'out of touch'.

Much criticism has been levelled in recent years at the organisational and structural features of social services departments since their reorganisation under the 1970 and 1974 Acts.[2] This has

Table 3.5   *Factors most undermining of social workers' effectiveness*

Undermining factors	Local authority social workers (% of total)	Probation Officers
Resources and facilities (including lack of finance)	25	16
Workload pressures		
general	13	14
lack of time	9	11
sub-total	22	25
Social workers'		
personal shortcomings generally	10	14
lack of professional skill, experience	8	4
sub-total	18	18
Staff shortages/difficulties	13	13
Organisation, structure, etc.	13	6
Role conflict/uncertainties	4	2
Other (including those relating to society)	6	11
None	13	20
No reply	4	6
TOTAL[1]	100	100
(number)	(1,220)	(203)

[1] Multiple replies.

recently been given an authoritative stamp in that one of the initiators of this reorganisation, Lord Seebohm, in an address to social workers, referred to the 'top-heavy' nature of social services departments.[3] 'Too much time', he said, 'was spent by social workers in administration and office meetings, and the salary and career structure of the social work profession should be revised [so that] those who stayed in contact with people should be paid more than administrators and managers.'

Such views would seem to be supported by not inconsiderable proportions of the respondents in this study. This sometimes took the form of dissatisfaction at being 'part of a bureaucracy which lacks dynamism and is always looking over its shoulder'. Sometimes, the feeling of being undermined by hierarchy was not focused only on social services departments—'the omnipresence of privilege', of 'stratification and ranking'—but also on 'every area and corner of our society, not least in the heart of our social work institutions'. The social workers' lack of autonomy or independence was ascribed by more than one respondent to a 'continual amalgamation into larger units'.

Role conflict or uncertainties were less often given as 'undermining' than as sources of dissatisfaction. Those who felt undermined by some aspect of role conflict or uncertainty included a hospital-based social worker, who found there was 'a lack of understanding about the social worker role by other hospital staff', as well as a social work assistant who complained of what she felt in her case to be 'responsibility without recognition'.

There is also considerable variation in viewpoint according to designation, with the partial exception of scarcity of resources to which all, except social work assistants, gave highest priority. Area management staff, for example, were more likely than other grades to feel undermined by problems arising from role conflict, seniors by organisational and structural factors, trainees by their own personal shortcomings, and fieldworkers by general pressures of work.

The fact that twice as many area management staff as any other group found that their effectiveness was undermined by factors relating to role conflict and uncertainties is of interest. This category of reply included references to the role of social services departments as well as to that of the individual social worker, and also to the 'demands' made upon them and their departments and to the esteem in which they are held. It is probable that area managers may be more exposed and thus more vulnerable than other grades to the impact of pressures from other agencies, their own central offices and government departments.

The Most Helpful Factor

In commenting on the factors which they felt were the most helpful to their effectiveness, local authority social workers and probation officers—men and women alike, though less often the younger members of the profession—tended to emphasise above all some aspect of their own personal qualities, sometimes referred to in such terms as their 'grim determination', or their 'own personality'. Others paid tribute to the support of their families, or stressed the value of their 'own upbringing' (Table 3.6). One in three local authority social workers, and two in five probation officers, evidently found such attributes a source of strength on which to draw in difficult or stressful situations—referring to them much more frequently than to their professional skills.

This finding is of some interest. First, it indicates that social workers are much more likely to find their personal strengths helpful than their personal weaknesses undermining. Secondly, when considered in the light of the rather small minorities in both samples who felt their professional skills and experience were the

Table 3.6   *Factors most helpful to social workers' effectiveness*

Helpful factors	Local authority social workers (% of total)	Probation officers
Social workers'		
personal qualities generally	30	39
professional skills, experience	10	10
sub-total	40	49
Support of colleagues	21	16
Adequacy of staff provision	11	5
Nature of workload, sufficient time, etc.	5	17
Organisation, structure, etc.	3	2
Resources, facilities	1	5
Other (including working conditions, pay etc)	4	6
None	16	16
No reply	4	6
TOTAL[1]	100	100
(number)	(1,220)	(203)

[1] Multiple replies.

most helpful factors, it would seem to reflect certain features of the training of social workers. It should be noted for example, that the unqualified social worker and newest recruit are more likely than the qualified and the experienced to feel undermined by their lack of professional skills or by their relative inexperience. The qualified and experienced social workers, on the other hand, are not more likely to refer to their professional expertise as the most helpful factor (except for those in senior and management posts). It is possible that underlying the nature of these responses is the emphasis, during formal professional training, or while gaining experience, on the importance of personal qualities on the job for fulfilling the professional task. Heraud (1970) has suggested for example, that the interpersonal nature of social work training marks it out from most other professional training in the sense that 'the primary instrument and skill' is the use of the 'self' of the caseworkers. In its attempts to redefine social work and to distinguish it from other forms of social service, the BASW Working Party (1977) attaches similar importance to the use of self, to personal skills and to the fact that the 'key resource is the social workers themselves'. Hence, the emphasis on personality characteristics, on 'the exploration of self', a process which, begun during formal training, continues under the day-to-day supervision of more senior and professional workers.

That substantial numbers of social workers commented on their personal rather than their professional strengths is possibly a result, therefore, of socialisation into the profession and of an important aspect of social work 'culture' becoming internalised. This would seem to be more marked among probation officers than among local authority social workers. Indeed, one probation officer thought that there was even more need for 'intensive work in social work training to help students to gain confidence in the use of *themselves* in social work'.

Next in order of importance as helpful factors were first, the support social workers felt they received from their colleagues and others ('friendly colleagues, who support one during periods of demoralisation and despondency'); and secondly, though to a lesser extent, the adequacy of back-up staff ('adequate and excellent clerical and administrative support', 'a very efficient secretary',) the provision of opportunities for discussion, in-service training and the like, and reasonably satisfactory working conditions.

Probation officers less often referred to such factors. They were more likely to feel helped by what they described as the satisfying nature of their work, by the time to do what they felt ought to be done, and by the composition of their caseloads. Such factors were very seldom referred to by local authority social workers.

Hardly any respondents, whether among local authority social workers or probation officers, thought that factors relating, for example, to the structure and organisation of their service, to resources and facilities, or to their working conditions, were particularly helpful to them. As many as one in six, judging from their replies, found nothing helpful to them.

More Undermined than Helped

Social workers clearly indicate that they are more likely to feel undermined by the lack of resources and facilities than helped by their availability. Equally, they find the nature of their workload, and the present structure and organisation of social services, more undermining than helpful. Moreover, some of the factors are said not only to undermine feelings of effectiveness in their work, but also their work satisfactions, and thus the hopes which originally motivated their entry into social work. Just under one-half for example, of the fieldworkers who see the scarcity of resources as an undermining factor also feel this scarcity is a major drawback to their satisfaction in casework. Of those who feel that their work pressures and insufficiency of time diminished their work satisfactions, over one-third also feel these same factors undermine their effectiveness.

By contrast, social workers find their support comes more often from their own personal strengths and qualities, and from the co-operation of their colleagues. There is thus a lack of balance in the elements that together constitute the provision of social work help. The implication would seem to be that, without the basic conditions for the practice of social work, social workers' personal assets can hardly be used to advantage. The chances are that they are dissipated to some degree in valiant but unavailing attempts to make up for more fundamental deficiencies in social service provision.

THE USE OF VOLUNTEERS

Any differences which emerged in social workers' motivations for entering social work, or in their satisfactions and dissatisfactions with their work, were not directly associated with the use of volunteers. Those who use volunteers are virtually indistinguishable from those who do not, where their attitudes and opinions on all these matters are concerned.

The explanation for this is presumably, as Chapter 9 shows, that the use of volunteers is not so much a function of attitudes as a function of workloads and, more specifically, of the size and composition of caseloads. Nevertheless, as we shall see, where volunteers are used to help with these caseloads, their use is only marginal in terms of the scale and scope of their deployment, the great bulk of work and responsibility being carried by the social workers themselves.

Attitudes may still be relevant, therefore, even though at this rather superficial level of inquiry no direct link with the use of volunteers may be traced. For the opinions of social workers in the present inquiry seem to express a set of hopes, beliefs and objectives which constitute, in the Halmos (1965) sense, a 'profession of faith' in their capacity to improve their own lives and those of others. Thus, most social workers seem to have set out to achieve self-realisation in their work, believing themselves capable of helping others and expecting thereby a relatively high degree of interpersonal involvement in the process.

This profession of faith (though by no means exclusive to social workers) may in itself serve to limit, if not in certain instances preclude, the intervention of those, such as volunteers, whose faiths may be of a different order. Moreover, social workers' hopes and beliefs are evidently sustained to the extent that their feelings of being useful and valued are confirmed by their day-to-day experiences. These, in many instances, are based on their relationships with their clients. Herein may lie yet another limitation, since the intervention of volunteers on any large scale may—in fact or fantasy—dilute these relationships.

The findings of the present inquiry are necessarily inconclusive on these matters, on which more intensive exploratory study is clearly required.

SUMMARY

Asked what they had hoped to achieve by entering social work, the great majority of respondents indicated that they were seeking some kind of self-fulfilment. This was to be achieved mainly through having a satisfying job as well as by helping others and, though to a lesser extent, by effecting some change in the lives of others or in the wider society. Respondents were less likely to recall what they had hoped to avoid by taking up social work, but of those who did describe their early hopes in this respect most, and particularly the younger age groups, had sought to avoid boring, routine, monotonous and otherwise unsatisfying work, often associated in their minds with occupations in industry or commerce and with objectives and values which they themselves did not support.

A major if not a principal source of satisfaction in working with clients at the present time—for local authority social workers and probation officers alike—is the feeling that they have contributed in different ways to bringing about some change for the better in their clients' situation and circumstances. A major drawback, however, at least for the local authority staff, is the scarcity of resources, including the lack of time. This is followed closely by the pressures and demands of their workloads. Both these factors are also cited as being the most undermining of social workers' feelings of effectiveness, though a sizeable minority also feel undermined by their own personal shortcomings. But if social workers find their personal weaknesses undermining, they also find that their personal strengths support them, in that these were more frequently cited as helpful to their effectiveness than were any other factors, including their professional skills. Though there is no apparent association between social workers' opinions on any of the above matters and their use of volunteers, nonetheless, their hopes and feelings about their careers and their work may have some bearing, albeit indirectly, on their attitudes towards volunteers and the use they make of their services.

NOTES

1 These two questions were used by Jeffreys (1965) in her survey of social welfare staff.
2 Local Authority Social Services Act, 1970; National Health Service Reorganisation Act, 1973.
3 Reported in *The Times*, 10 July 1976.

PART TWO SOCIAL WORKERS AND VOLUNTEERS

4 The Scale of Volunteer Use

INTRODUCTION

The growing interest in the use of volunteers in the statutory sector of the social services has not so far been matched with reliable information about the scale of this use. In many previous inquiries, the emphasis has tended to be on the study of voluntary workers and their activities or on the involvement of 'ordinary people' in voluntary work, usually in a local setting.[1] Rarely, if ever, has the link with the social workers themselves been explored. Little is known, therefore, of the number of social workers who use the services of volunteers for their clients at any one time, the number of volunteers involved, or the number of clients to whom they give their services.

It was one of the main objectives of the present study to try to remedy this. We hoped to collect the facts from which the incidence and scale of volunteer deployment in the statutory social services might be more realistically assessed.

In asking social workers about their use of volunteers' services, it was necessary first to define our meaning of the term 'volunteer' or 'voluntary worker'. Given the postal questionnaire method of investigation, no elaborate explanation could be used. A relatively simple definition, distilled from the many discussions about it held with individuals and groups during the exploratory phase, was finally used. Social workers were asked to consider in their replies all those volunteers providing a direct personal service, of whatever kind, to their clients. While still open to some misinterpretation, this effectively disqualified voluntary workers on committees, in community activities, fund-raising and the like. Some social workers, however, went further than our definition intended, and included in their replies volunteers who were receiving regular though nominal payments for their services or who were attached to a voluntary organisation providing an independent service, such as the Meals on Wheels Service. These volunteers, where specified, were not included in the analysis. It is possible that some such volunteers were not specified, but cross checks for consistency in social workers' replies suggest that there were relatively few in this category.

Secondly, we had to ensure that different categories of users and non-users could be distinguished. It was important, as we had established in the pilot study, not only to discover the proportion of social workers who had never worked with volunteers, but also the proportion who had at one time done so but no longer did. Similarly, in order that the nature of the relationships between social worker and volunteer might be explored, it was important to be able to distinguish social workers whose volunteers worked directly under their guidance from those whose volunteers did not. It was assumed that direct and indirect relationships between social workers and volunteers would be associated with the type of personal contact between them. This was confirmed in the subsequent analysis of respondents' answers concerning their contact with volunteers, described in Appendix III.

Social workers were asked, therefore, to indicate on the questionnaire which of several categories of relationship corresponded to their particular situation and, if they were using volunteers, to give the numbers concerned, and the number of clients these volunteers were helping.

INCIDENCE

The Local Authority Sample. Using the services of volunteers in one way or another is the current practice of just over one-half of local authority social workers, though a somewhat higher proportion are doing so amongst those who have caseloads. If this proportion approximates to that in the general social worker population of 25,000 in 1974, then it seems likely that about 13,000 social workers were, at the time of inquiry, working with volunteers in the local authority setting.

This picture has two important aspects. First, the most typical relationship between professionals and volunteers in local authority social services departments is that where the volunteers are not, on the whole, in close or regular contact with the social workers whose clients they help. As Table 4.1 shows, the great majority of those working with volunteers are involved in what we term an indirect relationship, characterised by relatively infrequent contact between the two parties or none at all.

Only one in three of those involved with volunteers have what we defined as a direct relationship with all or with some of their volunteers, this being characterised by a much higher degree of personal contact between social worker and volunteer at each stage of their collaboration.

Secondly, social workers without any experience whatsoever of working with volunteers are relatively few, the largest category of non-users consisting of social workers who once used the services of volunteers but no longer do so. As will be seen, one reason for this is that the movement of social workers into positions of

Table 4.1   *The use of volunteers' services*

| Type of relationship | Local authority social workers | | Probation officers |
	Total	Caseload[1] holders only (% of total)	
Users			
volunteers under social workers' guidance			
indirect	34	37	10
indirect and direct	12	13	21
direct	5	6	39
sub-total	51	56	70
Non-users			
not now using volunteers	33	30	21
never have used volunteers	14	14	9
sub-total	47	44	30
No reply	2	–	–
TOTAL	100	100	100
(number)	(1,220)	(888)	(203)

[1] Excluding hospital-based social workers.

seniority and management is associated with a reduction and changes in caseloads, or with giving them up altogether.

The result is that the incidence of volunteer use varies considerably according to seniority. Less than one in five area management staff for example, use volunteers compared with twice as many seniors and three times as many fieldworkers who do so. The incidence among senior social workers is thus well below the mean. Volunteer use is highest of all among social work assistants and a little higher than average among trainees. It is also evident that the more senior designations represent the smallest proportions of social workers who have never used volunteers, but the highest proportions who at one time used them but no longer do so.

When those who do not have caseloads are excluded from the analysis, however, the differences between the designations in their use of volunteers virtually disappear, except that, again, a much higher proportion of social work assistants than of others—nearly three-quarters—are using volunteers (Table 4.2). Moreover, while indirect relationships with volunteers predominate for everyone, it is the social work assistants who are the most likely to have such relationships with their voluntary workers. Senior social workers and fieldworkers, on the other hand, are more likely than others to work directly with their volunteers, either with all or some of them.

Indeed, for seniors the direct is almost as frequent as the indirect relationship, so that they are much more evenly balanced between the two main types of relationship with volunteers than other social workers.

Table 4.2   *The use of volunteers according to designation;*
caseload holders only: local authority social workers

Type of relationship	Area officers/ deputies	Senior social workers	Field workers (% of total)	Train- ees	Social work assis- tants	Total
Users	*Number*					
volunteers under social workers' guidance						
indirect	(8)	28	34	43	56	37
indirect and direct	(4)	12	15	13	12	13
direct	(1)	12	6	2	4	6
sub-total	(13)	52	55	58	72	56
Non-users						
not now using volunteers	(15)	43	29	26	11	30
never have used volunteers	(3)	5	16	16	17	14
sub-total	(18)	48	45	42	28	44
TOTAL[1]	..	100	100	100	100	100
(number)	(31)	(108)	(583)	(61)	(104)	(887)

[1] Excluding no replies.

The Probation Sample. Three interesting features distinguish probation officers from social workers in their use of volunteers (Table 4.1). First, among the probation officers a considerably higher proportion (seven in ten) is currently using the services of volunteers. Secondly, a much higher proportion (almost two-fifths) is involved in the direct, more personal type of relationship with their voluntary workers. Indeed, the pattern of relationships between professionals and volunteers in this particular respect is markedly different for the two samples. The third distinguishing feature relates to the non-users, of whom proportionately fewer than in the local authority services have never used the services of volunteers. Experience of working with volunteers thus extends even more widely among probation officers than among local authority social workers.

There seem to be a number of reasons for these quite distinctive

differences. Of considerable importance, undoubtedly, is the influence of central policy in the probation service since 1965, which has
actively encouraged the use of volunteers (Cmnd 3107, 1965;
Clarke, 1975; Reading 1967). The data suggest, however, that
underlying some of these differences may be factors which origin-
ate in the nature of the roles and responsibilities of the staff in each
type of service, in the composition of their clientele, and in the type
of social work intervention that each service requires. These
matters are discussed in more detail in Chapter 12. At this stage, it
is enough to point out that the status or seniority of social workers
in the local authority services, the size and composition of their
caseloads, and the fact that those in senior positions are less likely
to have caseloads at all, appear to be the main factors affecting
their use of volunteers.

Variations Between Local Authority Social Services Departments
Though it was not possible to assess the variations between local
authority areas in the incidence of volunteer use for the country as
a whole, the variation among the areas covered in the present
inquiry suggests that such differences may be general.

At one extreme, as many as four in five of the respondents in one
authority area were using voluntary help, while at the other no
more than one in six were doing so. The differences are much
smaller when authorities are grouped by administrative types, the
incidence of volunteer use being somewhat lower, on average, in
the five metropolitan districts than in the eight counties or in the six
London boroughs (since there were only two Scottish regions, these
were excluded from the analysis).[2]

It was thought of interest to examine the characteristics of the
respondents for each authority covered so as to trace which factors,
if any, might underlie these variations. The analysis reveals first,
that just as there were considerable differences among authorities
in the incidence of volunteer use, so there were in most other
respects. Thus, the age structure, the ratio of women to men, the
proportions of qualified social workers and of BASW members,
the average length of experience, the average caseload size, and the
structure of social work staff all show considerable variations
between different authorities. Since the sample of respondents is, in
many of the above respects, generally representative of the social
worker population as a whole, this suggests that there is little
uniformity in the personnel of local authority social services
departments. The BASW Report (1977) also draws attention to the
lack of uniformity in the deployment of staff in social services
departments across the country, particularly as shown in the nature
of the job descriptions for social work personnel and in the
underlying philosophies of the departments themselves. This

presumably reflects each authority's particular staff policies and procedures, the size of its personnel, its demographic features, the characteristics of its environment, as well as the effects of recent local government reorganisation.

The analysis also shows that most of the differences considered were not associated in any way with variations in the incidence of volunteer use, the two exceptions being the number of social work personnel employed in each authority and the staff structure. The four authorities with the lowest incidence of volunteer use were compared with the four authorities with the highest. This showed first, that the average number of social workers employed was smaller where the incidence of volunteer use was lowest (82 per authority) than where it was highest (240 per authority). Secondly, the proportion of social workers employed in area management was three times as high in the authorities with the lowest incidence of volunteer use as in the authorities with the highest. The latter finding is certainly consistent with the general tendency for volunteers to be less often used by management staff, mainly, as will be seen, because a relatively high proportion of them do not have caseloads.

SCALE

The evidence of the present inquiry suggests that when social workers work with volunteers they do so on a relatively small scale. Most of the social workers who use volunteers, it seems, are not likely to work with more than a few volunteers at any one time, or to use their services for more than a few of their clients.

The Local Authority Sample. It proved difficult to establish the precise scale on which voluntary help was being used. The chief problem was that of the 400 or so local authority social workers whose volunteers were not under their direct guidance. Substantial proportions either did not give the numbers of volunteers and clients involved or said they did not know. Added to this, there was no way of knowing the extent of duplication in the numbers reported.

Given these difficulties, it was decided to use as the basis for assessing the possible scale of operation the replies of respondents who were in a direct relationship with their volunteers, among whom there were fewer invalid replies concerning numbers. There also seemed to be a reason for assuming little, if any, duplication where the more direct and personal contact with volunteers applied.

On this basis, it seems that just over one-half of the direct users are involved with one or two volunteers, though substantial proportions are working with between three to five. Fewer, however, are working with more than this. There is a similar, though not identical, pattern for the number of clients helped by volunteers. Though the largest single group of social workers—over one-quarter—use volunteers for only one of their cases, as many as one-fifth involve their volunteers with between three and five. A further quarter have volunteers attached to six or more of their clients. Clients being helped thus outnumber volunteers.

The Probation Sample. It was possible to estimate the scale of volunteer use in the probation service more accurately than in the local authority services. For one thing, as already noted, the proportion involved in a direct relationship with their volunteers is much higher among probation officers. Moreover, fewer of the replies of the indirect users in the probation service were invalid. The resulting analysis shows that, in spite of a markedly higher incidence of volunteer use, the scale of use appears to be no larger than in the local authority services. Thus, similarly higher proportions—nearly two-thirds—of the direct users are working with only one or two volunteers, and smaller proportions with more than six. A similar pattern was evident for indirect users.

The number of clients helped is on an even smaller scale than among local authority social workers, so that just under one-half are using volunteers for one or two of their cases. Also, unlike the local authority sample, the one-to-one match between volunteers and cases predominates.

Our findings tend to confirm, therefore, what others have assumed to be the case (Darvill, 1975), namely that, on a purely quantitative level, working with volunteers in the statutory services is a small-scale operation, in terms of the numbers of volunteers and clients involved.

It is by no means clear how far this scale of things is determined by such factors as the supply of 'suitable' volunteers or of 'suitable' clients, particularly since the criteria for assessing the suitability of either are highly subjective. Another important factor influencing the outcome, at least for the direct users of volunteers, may be the capacity of social workers, given the demands of their workloads, to collaborate with more than one or two voluntary workers at a time, or to share any but a few of their clients with them. There is not only the fact that the effective use of volunteers' services requires the expenditure of time and effort but, as the Aves Committee (1969) pointed out, the use of volunteers often brings to light difficulties which require more, rather than less, professional care. Thus the use of volunteers may lead to greater demands on social workers' time. The scale of volunteer use as revealed in the present inquiry, therefore, may represent a more feasible level of volunteer use in present circumstances than might be achieved by policies aimed at a higher recruitment of voluntary workers into the statutory services.

If the existing scale of volunteer use, at least by the direct users, represents, as it may, these social workers' limits concerning their capacity to use volunteers in the context of their current work, then to attempt to increase the scale of operations among those already committed to a personal relationship with their volunteers may push them beyond these limits, with counter-productive results.

Nor may it necessarily be assumed that higher levels of recruitment could be achieved amongst indirect users. Here, too, there may be limitations, not the least important being a reluctance to allocate more than a few cases to voluntary helpers with whom the professional may have only tenuous links.

National Estimates

These results can be used to make a very approximate estimate of the aggregate of volunteers and of the individuals they aid and support over the country as a whole. A conservative estimate, based on the assumption that the incidence and scale of volunteer use is similar for the general social worker population as for the sample of respondents, suggests that the total number of volunteers involved with social workers employed by local authorities in Great Britain is probably about 40,000-45,000 and the number of individuals helped by them at any one time may be in the region of 65,000-70,000.[3] The estimated number of social workers involved, as we have seen, would be about 13,000. In the probation service, the corresponding numbers in England and Wales may approximate to 10,000 volunteers though a recent survey suggests that only 3,400 of these are accredited Voluntary Associates (Clarke, 1975), helping over 13,000 clients for just over 3,800 probation officers.

SUMMARY

Just over one-half of local authority social workers and seven-tenths of probation officers are working with volunteers. The most typical relationship between social workers and volunteers in the local authority services is one where the volunteers do not work under the direct guidance of the social worker, and where there is little, if any, personal contact between them. In the probation service, the most typical relationship is a direct one characterised by close and regular personal contact. There are marked variations between different designations in the use of volunteers, social work assistants being the most likely to use them.

Substantial minorities in both samples once used the services of volunteers but no longer do so. Relatively few social workers have never worked with volunteers, so that the experience of drawing upon voluntary help extends fairly widely.

There was considerable variation in the incidence of volunteer use as between the local authority departments taking part in the survey. The characteristics of the sample of social workers also varied from authority to authority as did aspects of staff structure. The incidence of volunteer use, however, appeared to be lower in the smaller social services offices, and where there were proportionately more social workers in management posts.

As far as can be assessed from the data, when social workers use volunteers they do so on a relatively small scale, most of them working with one or two. The numbers of clients helped is on a similar scale, though, in general, these exceed the numbers of volunteers.

Estimates suggest that in the general social worker population there may be nearly 13,000 local authority social workers using at least 40,000 volunteers, helping nearly 70,000 clients. In the probation service, the corresponding estimates are nearly 4,000 probation officers, working with some 10,000 volunteers, who are helping over 13,000 clients.

NOTES

1 See for instance, special studies quoted in the Aves Report (1969), e.g.: Mary Morris *A Study of Halifax and London* for the National Council of Social Service (1965); *A Survey of the Preparation and Training of Voluntary Workers in the City of Manchester* Manchester and Salford Council of Social Service and Manchester Youth and Community Service (1967); *Voluntary Workers in Liverpool* Department of Adult Education, Liverpool University (1967); *Voluntary Workers in Six Organisations* Institute of Community Studies (1967).

2 Though the mean proportion of volunteer use for the sample as a whole is 58 per cent, this has a standard deviation as high as 16.5 per cent (co-efficient of variation 28.4 per cent). Among the authorities in each category there are considerable variations, the standard deviation of the series being between 12.5 and 13.4, and the co-efficient of variation being highest in the metropolitan districts and lowest in the counties.

3 The estimates of the numbers of voluntary workers in Britain in the Report of the Wolfenden Committee (1977), and discussed in *New Society* (Hatch and Mocroft 7 April 77), are not comparable with those presented in the present inquiry. In the Wolfenden Report, voluntary workers were defined much more widely than in our study. In general, they covered committee workers and fund-raisers and, in the statutory sector, workers in schools, youth clubs, day centres of various kinds and the like. Moreover, in the Wolfenden study, the individuals engaged—directly or indirectly—in providing services for the clients of the social worker staff of the statutory personal social services could not be precisely identified. Their numbers, therefore, could not be accurately estimated. The evidence suggests, however, that they represent an extremely small fraction of all the voluntary workers covered in the study.

5 Working with Volunteers

INTRODUCTION

Three main aspects of working with volunteers are described in this chapter. First—briefly and in broad terms—we sketch the kinds of activities undertaken by the volunteers who assist social workers in the statutory services. Secondly, we discuss the reasons given by social workers for using the services of volunteers in these activities. Thirdly, we seek to describe—again broadly—the patterns of collaboration between the professional and the volunteer, particularly the kind of personal contact between them.

VOLUNTARY ACTIVITIES

Many studies of voluntary activities have shown how varied are the tasks and types of work undertaken by voluntary workers.[1] The range is indeed so wide as often to present difficulties of analysis and classification for research purposes. In the present inquiry, therefore, we decided to anticipate such difficulties by classifying voluntary activities into five main groups. These correspond in modified form to the broad divisions drawn up in the Aves Committee Report (1969). For us, as for the Committee, the divisions themselves do not imply any order of usefulness in the activities concerned.

Respondents were asked to indicate upon which of the following types of service their volunteers were mainly engaged:

(a) practical tasks, e.g. escorting, gardening, transport, decorating, etc;
(b) work requiring special skills other than that of social work, e.g. nursing, crafts, legal aid;
(c) befriending, routine visiting, etc;
(d) counselling;
(e) other (to be specified by the respondent).

We had a limited aim here—to discover how many social workers were using volunteers in each of the above types of service. Owing to the wide scope of the inquiry it was not possible to cover other aspects of the volunteers' activities, such as their frequency, the amount of time spent on them or the number of volunteers engaged in them.

The Local Authority Sample. Social workers' replies show clearly enough that there are two main categories of activity for which they are most likely to use volunteers (Table 5.1). The first of these is befriending. Almost two in three social workers deploy their volunteers on this type of service. The second, involving almost as many social workers, is work of a practical kind. Far fewer social workers are evidently drawing on voluntary help for activities which require special skills, for counselling, or for other types of activity specified by the respondents themselves, such as group or community work.

Table 5.1 *Proportion of social workers using volunteers for different types of service*

Main type of service	Local authority social workers (% of total)	Probation officers
Befriending	65	80
Practical tasks	59	31
Work requiring special skills	10	16
Counselling	6	15
Other	13	14
No reply	2	—
TOTAL[1]	100	100
(number)	(623)	(141)

[1] Multiple replies.

None of these activities is mutually exclusive, since, as Darvill (1975) argues, 'it is hard to judge where chores end and friendship begins'. While a precise picture of volunteer deployment could not be obtained from our data, it is evident that some social workers are using volunteers over the whole spectrum of activity, and many on more than one type of task.

It is also evident that while the type of relationship that many social workers have with their volunteers—direct or indirect—hardly seems to be associated with the way they use them, designation and caseload size do seem to have this association. Thus, seniors are more likely than fieldworkers to use volunteers on counselling activities, while social work assistants are less likely to use them on activities requiring special skills. Similarly, as caseload size rises, so do the proportions of social workers using volunteers on practical and befriending activities, whereas the proportion of social workers using them for counselling activities falls. These tendencies may reflect not only differences in approach to the use of volunteers but differences in caseload composition.

The Probation Sample. The probation service, in its deployment of volunteers, presents a very different picture from that of the local authority services, presumably as a result of its more specialised functions. Proportionately more probation officers are using volunteers for befriending and counselling activities—involving them in personal relationships generally—and far fewer for practical tasks, compared with local authority social workers (Table 5.1).

Moreover, there appear to be quite sharp differences in how volunteers are used according to the type of relationship probation officers have with them. It is the probation staff in a direct relationship with their volunteers who are the most likely to use them on services where the personal element takes precedence over the more practical. By contrast, probation officers, whose volunteers do not work under their direct guidance, are evidently more likely to use them for work requiring special skills.

CLIENTS HELPED

The Local Authority Sample. It is widely believed that some services, such as those for elderly people, use more volunteers than others. We thought it important in the present inquiry to discover the extent to which such beliefs were valid. Respondents were accordingly asked to indicate which client groups were being helped by their voluntary workers. Certain difficulties arose in defining each client group in terms that were meaningful and acceptable to social workers. A final list of fifteen groups was evolved on the basis of consultation with other research workers as well as with the personnel of some social services departments.[2] The analysis of probation officers' replies is not given here since, as was to be expected, their volunteers are used predominantly (though not exclusively) for prisoners, their families, adults before the courts, and so on.

As Table 5.2 shows, elderly people are indeed among the most frequently cited by social workers as being helped by their volunteers, but virtually as many are using voluntary help for their physically handicapped clients.[3] Thus, more than twice as many social workers are using volunteers for these two client groups (over two in five) as for children, blind people or those with mental illnesses. Even fewer social workers allocate their volunteers to any other client group.

This pattern of volunteer deployment varies slightly according to the type of relationship social workers have with their volunteers and according to their designation. Thus, social workers in a direct relationship with their volunteers are more likely than others to use them for cases involving children, but less likely for clients who are deaf or mentally handicapped. Similarly, senior social workers

Table 5.2 *Proportion of social workers allocating
volunteers to different client groups*

Client group	Local authority social workers (% of total)
Elderly (unimpaired)	44
Physically handicapped	43
Blind	21
Children	20
Mentally ill	19
Families with varied problems	17
Mentally handicapped	14
Physically ill	12
Deaf	11
Individuals with varied problems	8
Homeless	6
Children before the courts/panels	4
Adults before the courts	2
Fostering/adoption	2
Other	4
No reply	1
TOTAL[1]	100
(number)	(623)

[1] Multiple replies.

more often use their volunteers for children than for elderly or handicapped people. Again, such tendencies seem to reflect differences in approach and in caseload composition.

THE ACTIVITIES AND THE CLIENTS

In order to obtain more precise information about different types of activity or client group, social workers were asked to describe in their own words the nature of the help given in the last instance a volunteer had helped a client new to them. From these descriptions, it was evident that a new category of voluntary service needed to be distinguished. Some volunteers were described as helping clients on a deeper level than is indicated by the term 'befriending', though the help given did not appear to involve the kind of skills implied by that of 'counselling'. Since we recognised the difficulty of judging where befriending ends and counselling begins, we decided to classify this category of help as 'personal support'. About one in eight volunteers were said to have provided this kind of support when they last helped a new client.

Several points of interest emerged from the examination of volunteers' activities in the last instance. First, there is a fairly close correspondence between these activities and social workers'

Table 5.3   *Activities undertaken by volunteers in the last instance*

Type of activity	Local authority social workers (% of total)
Practical tasks	47
Befriending	41
Personal support	12
Group or club activities	5
Work requiring special skills	5
Counselling	1
Other	12
No reply	6
TOTAL[1]	100
(Number)	(597)

[1] Multiple replies.

references to the way they use volunteers generally. Thus, the most recent activities described tended again to be mostly of a practical and befriending kind, whilst the client groups most often helped were first, elderly people, then, less often, those with physical handicaps, individuals and families with varied problems including homelessness, and children (Tables 5.3 and 5.4).[4] Similarly, in the probation service volunteers were mainly engaged in befriending and in giving personal support to clients. Here, however, far fewer in proportion were giving practical help.

Secondly, it is evident that the activities undertaken in the local authority services do vary according to who is helped. As can be

Table 5.4   *Client groups helped by volunteers in the last instance*

Client group	Local authority social workers (% of total)
Elderly (unimpaired)	24
Physically handicapped	14
Individuals and families with varied problems, including homelessness	13
Children	10
Physically ill	4
Mentally ill	4
Mentally handicapped	3
Others	6
Unspecified	35
No reply	15
TOTAL[1]	100
(number)	(597)

[1] Multiple replies.

seen from Table 5.5, elderly and physically handicapped people were more likely than others to receive practical help and befriending visits, while individuals and families facing a variety of problems, and children, were more likely to receive personal support and help. Moreover, the latter supportive help was more often given by volunteers who were working under the direct guidance of the social workers. Generally, most of the activities described extended to all client groups, though in varying degrees. Tasks requiring special skills, providing links with the social services, or related to financial aid, however, were rarely undertaken by volunteers.

Table 5.5 *Client group helped and activities undertaken by volunteers in the last instance: local authority social workers*

Selected type of activity	Elderly (unimpaired)	Physically handicapped	Individuals and families with varied problems[1] (% of total)	Children
Practical	53	54	27	37
Befriending	51	43	36	35
Personal support	4	7	30	19
TOTAL[2]	100	100	100	100
(number)	(81)	(78)	(54)	(141)

[1] Including homelessness.
[2] Multiple replies.

Thirdly, there were noticeable differences in the sex and age of volunteers in the local authority sample according to the types of activity they had undertaken and the client groups they had helped. Thus, men were more likely than women to have given practical services, and women more likely than men to have given befriending services or to have helped the elderly. These tendencies were more marked, if anything, among the volunteers who were not working under the direct guidance of their social workers.

In terms of the age differences among volunteers, the under-18s were more often involved in practical activities but, in turn, were less often involved than older volunteers with children, with individuals and families, or, when working directly for social workers, in befriending clients.

It is difficult to deduce from the data how much choice social workers have in respect of the age of volunteers when allocating tasks to volunteers. In both services women predominated, but among volunteers in the local authority services there were rather more volunteers, proportionately, under the age of 30 than there were over the age of 50, the average age being virtually the same as for the social worker sample—just under 38 years. In the probation sample, the age distribution of volunteers follows a rather different pattern. There were no volunteers under the age of 18, for example, and rather higher proportions under the age of 30. Volunteers in the statutory services, therefore, may not entirely match the middle-aged image. They are, however, nearer to the 'typical' volunteer found in other studies in being mainly women.[5]

In the light of our findings, social workers' use of volunteers in the local authority setting seems to conform to expectations. In other words, volunteers are mainly women. They are used predominantly for visiting, befriending and helping out clients in practical ways. The clients, for the most part, are elderly or physically handicapped. The voluntary worker in the local authority services is, as Darvill (1975) observes, 'rarely used for intensive long-term involvement with the more demanding clients'.

Clearly there are a number of factors which influence these patterns. Some of these—such as the link between the representation of elderly and physically handicapped people in referrals and caseloads—are discussed in Chapter 9. Another factor is presumably the type of social work intervention that clients are thought to need, or that is considered feasible in the circumstances. There is also the extent to which volunteers are believed to be the most suitable resource for providing the kind of extra or necessary help that social workers consider should be given.

Certainly there is a high degree of correspondence between local authority social workers' actual use of volunteers and their beliefs as to what are the most suitable activities for them. Volunteers do what social workers believe they ought to do and largely on the basis of a division of labour which differentiates the respective functions of the professional and the voluntary worker much more sharply than in the probation service. It is interesting to note that the client groups most often helped by volunteers in the local authority services—elderly and physically handicapped people—are not those with whom social workers themselves, given the choice, would most prefer to work. Among the most preferred groups for social workers are children and then families with various problems, each of whom tend to be less likely than other client groups to be helped by volunteers.

It would be misleading, however, to interpret this as meaning that social workers necessarily allocate volunteers to cases that they themselves have no strong liking for, since no one-to-one comparison between their preferences and their use of volunteers was made. It would seem to reflect preferences of a different kind. As will be seen later, social workers show a stronger preference for ongoing casework, where they feel they may effect some change in the individual or in the situation, than for the kinds of supportive services and practical aid which have come to be associated with social work for elderly and handicapped people. Presumably, if volunteers are able to take on these supportive tasks, social workers see themselves as partially released to use their skills in the direction of their preferences and for the tasks which, if qualified, they feel they have been trained. This was evident in the reasons they gave for using volunteers.

REASONS FOR USING VOLUNTEERS

The reasons why social workers use voluntary help in the ways described may seem self-evident from what has gone before. Yet we thought that it was important to try and obtain rather fuller accounts as to why they used volunteers in these different ways. We thus hoped to discover how far voluntary help was seen as a means of achieving different ends, or as having some intrinsic value in itself.

The Local Authority Sample. Many social workers gave their reasons in considerable detail, a substantial number offering more than one reason, and some describing in enthusiastic terms the help voluntary workers gave, without which, according to one respondent, the social services would be 'non-viable'.

As Table 5.6 shows, three main groups of reasons for using voluntary help were found to predominate. First, because it provides specified benefits—both practical and personal—to clients. Over one-half of the social workers were of this view. Of these benefits, the practical aspects were more often emphasised (though by proportionately far fewer senior social workers) through references to such activities or 'chores' as gardening, shopping, household maintenance and repairs of different kinds. The personal benefits derived by clients from voluntary help, however, were noted by nearly one-quarter of the social workers, who described volunteers as a 'source of help and comfort', with time 'to befriend'. One respondent wrote that 'loneliness is often worse than illness'. Another stressed a client's response to the non-professional, and the deep impression made by anyone who was 'prepared to care enough for them personally to give their time voluntarily in an effort to help'.

Secondly, almost one in three social workers thought that volunteers represented a special resource. Typical of the comments of this group were the references to volunteers providing 'a different quality of relationship', and 'a better and more imaginative service'. Again, in some circumstances, the advantages of the non-professional and the non-authority figure were stressed, the

Table 5.6   *Reasons for using volunteers*

Reasons	Local authority social workers (% of total)	Probation officers
Benefits to clients		
practical	32	18
personal	23	49
sub-total	55	67
A special resource	31	36
Benefits for social worker	30	31
Benefits for community	4	7
Other	3	4
No reply	8	5
TOTAL[1]	100	100
(number)	(623)	(141)

[1] Multiple replies.

volunteer being seen as someone who often has 'an insight into clients' problems' not always possible, evidently, in the professional relationship.

Thirdly, nearly as many social workers (though far fewer social work assistants) emphasised the benefits that voluntary help brings to social workers themselves. Volunteers could 'release social work staff from the routine support tasks that a volunteer can do equally well—visiting, shopping, transporting, etc.'—or, as another commented, 'provide service, time and social contact' that the social worker could not provide herself. Some social workers stressed the saving of time when volunteers were used, allowing the professionals to devote themselves to the more demanding cases. Others saw volunteers as supporting and supplementing their role, not only saving time but 'filling the gaps', sometimes in their own capabilities, as with one social worker who, being a young man, felt unable to fulfil a client's 'need for a grandmother figure'!

Fourthly, there are the social workers, and particularly senior staff, who use volunteers because they feel there is some gain thereby to the community. These were small in number in spite of current fashions in community-oriented ideas. They reflected nevertheless distinctive views on such matters as the principles of self-help and of community involvement. In every community, according to one social worker, 'there are people in need of help, and people—not professionals—who are willing to help and who have the time and enthusiasm to do so'. This social worker believed 'strongly in the self-help idea', and was against social workers being 'all things to all people' when 'there are people in the community who are often more able to help on particular tasks than we'. Another social worker took the view that volunteers represented the community as 'a token of acceptance of rejected and alienated people'.

Summing up, many social workers seem to have an instrumental approach to the use of volunteers, seeing them as the means of achieving particular objectives, mostly to the advantage of clients but also of themselves. This same approach has been noted by Darvill in his attempts to classify social workers' attitudes towards volunteers. It is exemplified in his definition of the 'suburban' attitude where social workers seem to require an 'obedient, cheap and above all respectable service', and of the 'au pair' attitude where, though the volunteer is closely involved in the domestic life of social services departments, this is only on the basis of 'the performance of the most basic chores'. A minority, but a substantial one, evidently used volunteers in an expressive context, seeing in their freely offered services an intrinsic value in its own right. Some combined both approaches in their replies.

The Probation Sample. Generally, probation officers' reasons for using volunteers tend to follow a similar pattern to those of social workers. The main differences are first, that rather more probation officers referred to the benefits that clients derive from voluntary help and secondly, that they put much greater emphasis on the personal than on the practical gains from using voluntary help.

PATTERNS OF COLLABORATION

In Chapter 4, we distinguished social workers according to their direct and indirect relationships with volunteers. We wished, however, to explore further the nature of these relationships. We wanted to know the extent to which volunteers working under the direct guidance of social workers were in close or regular contact with them, and how far an indirect relationship precluded any such personal contact. It also seemed to us that one indicator of the professionals' investment of time and energy in voluntary activities might well be the closeness and regularity of their contact with the volunteers in question.

Accordingly, we asked respondents about three stages in the process of enlisting voluntary help during the last instance a volunteer had helped a new client. We asked them who had made the initial approach; who had explained what had to be done; and who had provided the necessary guidance, support and supervision, and how regularly.

On the matter of supervision, we recognised the difficulty of finding a satisfactory term for the kind of 'oversight given by responsible persons' which is often felt to be necessary where volunteers undertake work of a highly personal nature (Aves, 1969). We partially resolved the problem by using questions adapted from the Aves Committee study, which specified the nature of the responsibility carried by the volunteer, the regularity of their reporting back and to whom they reported.

At the first stage of approaching volunteers for their help, it is evident that indirect relationships by no means exclude some degree of personal contact between the social workers and the volunteers concerned. Though over one-half of direct users personally contacted volunteers to ask for their help, over one-quarter of indirect users did likewise (Table 5.7). Among the indirect users, however, volunteers were almost as likely to have been approached by an outside agency. This rarely occurred among the direct users. Persons with special responsibility for volunteers at area office level also played some part in approaching volunteers, and about one-quarter of social workers, direct and indirect users alike, used this particular intermediary. There was apparently little, if any, variation in the type of approach to volunteers according to the nature of the task they were asked to do or to the type of client they were asked to help.

Table 5.7   *Initial approach to volunteer in the last instance*

Approach made by	Local authority social workers			Probation officers
	Direct users	Indirect users	Total	
		(% of total)		
Social worker	53	29	35	36
Person responsible for volunteers in area or central office	30	34	33	49
Outside agency	4	25	19	3
Other	13	12	12	12
No reply	1	1	1	1
TOTAL[1]	100	100	100	100
(number)	(156)	(441)	(597)	(141)

[1] Multiple replies.

There was a much higher incidence of personal contact between social workers and volunteers, however, at the stage of explaining the nature of the task to the volunteer than at the initial stage (Table 5.8). The differences between the direct and indirect users, however, were still very marked. Almost nine in ten direct users explained personally to their volunteers what was required, compared with just over two-fifths of the indirect users. Moreover, other intermediaries, including any staff members specially appointed or delegated with responsibility for volunteers as well as the outside agency, played a very minor role for direct users compared with indirect users, over one-half of whom relied on one or other of these intermediaries for explaining to the volunteer the kind of help required.

Table 5.8 *Explanation to volunteer in the last instance*

Explanation by	Local authority social workers			Probation officers
	Direct users	Indirect users (% of total)	Total	
Social worker	87	44	56	82
Person responsible for volunteers	11	27	23	13
Other member of staff	5	5	5	5
Outside agency	1	24	18	1
Other	1	5	4	4
No reply	1	1	1	1
TOTAL[1]	100	100	100	100
(number)	(156)	(441)	(597)	(141)

[1] Multiple replies.

Finally, at what may loosely be called the supervisory stage, there were again differences between social workers according to the type of relationship they had with their volunteers (Table 5.9). By definition, it was the personal supervision by the workers themselves which distinguished the direct from the indirect relationship. This did not necessarily mean close supervision, which, indeed applied only to a minority. More usually, volunteers in direct relationships were supervised through regular reporting back to the social worker.

Volunteers in indirect relationships with their social workers are also likely to be supervised. But in their case the supervision is by others—such as a colleague, a person in the office responsible for volunteers, or someone in an outside agency. These volunteers are more likely than others, however, to be working on their own, reporting back only when in difficulty. Generally, it is not their level of responsibility that distinguishes the relationship of volunteers with social workers, but the fact that volunteers in the indirect type of relationship are far less likely to be personally supervised by the social workers themselves.

Thus, during the whole process of enlisting the help of the volunteer, indirect users are far less often in contact with the volunteer than the direct users. At no stage, however, do indirect

Table 5.9   *Supervision of volunteer in the last instance*

| Type of supervision | Local authority social workers | | | Probation officers |
	Direct users	Indirect users (% of total)	Total	
Volunteer carries responsibility and reports back only when in difficulty	26	36	33	16
reports back regularly to:				
social worker	55	15	25	66
colleague or person responsible for volunteers	6	18	15	6
outside agency	–	18	13	1
works under close supervision of:				
social worker	15	–	4	7
colleague and person responsible for volunteers	2	7	6	1
outside agency	–	10	7	–
Other	3	2	2	4
No reply	1	1	1	1
TOTAL[1]	100	100	100	100
(number)	(156)	(441)	(597)	(141)

[1] Multiple replies.

relationships exclude some social workers from a degree of personal contact with the volunteers concerned, though it seems that in many instances there is no personal contact at all. Both indirect and direct users are most likely to be personally involved with volunteers in the explanation of what has to be done. This suggests that many social workers regarded their intervention at this stage as being more important than at others. Personal involvement at the supervisory stage is evidently next in importance for direct users, followed by the stage of initial approach. The reverse order applies to indirect users, the least frequent contact being at the supervisory stage.

It does not seem that social workers' contacts with volunteers are influenced in any substantial way by the nature of the help required or by the individual who needs the help, except in two particular respects. First, social workers, especially the indirect users, are more likely themselves to explain to volunteers what has to be done where personal support at a rather more complex level than befriending is required, but less likely to do so where elderly people are concerned. Secondly, where volunteers are involved in more personal relationships with clients, particularly with children and families, social workers are more likely to give them personal and regular supervision and guidance.

The Probation Sample. Probation officers are much more likely than local authority staff to use a specialist officer for contacting the volunteer, and much higher proportions of them personally explain what has to be done and personally supervise the volunteers concerned. The latter reflects the higher incidence in the probation officers' sample of direct and more personal relationships with volunteers (Tables 5.7, 5.8 and 5.9). In this respect, therefore, local authority social workers whose volunteers work under their direct guidance are much nearer in their patterns of collaboration with volunteers to the typical model in the probation sample.

The evidence thus suggests that direct relationships are characterised by a closer and more regular personal contact between the professional and the volunteer, and that consequently the investment of professional capital is higher in these relationships. Such investment is clearly lower in the local authority services than in the probation service.

A TENTATIVE CONCLUSION

It is difficult to know whether the patterns of volunteer deployment described here[6] represent the kind of development that was hoped for with the reorganisation and restructuring of the social services. The findings of the present inquiry, however, suggest that in two important respects—in the scope of the volunteers' activities and in the nature of the relationships between social workers and volunteers—earlier hopes may not have been realised. First, it seems that the services volunteers carry out have not yet broadened out sufficiently to lessen the emphasis on befriending and practical help to handicapped and elderly people, which has for so long characterised voluntary effort in general, whoever its sponsors.

Secondly, most local authority social workers who are using the services of volunteers for their clients seem not to be working closely with them; many have no personal contact with them at all. Close collaboration between social workers and volunteers in the local authority setting is not typical.

Subsequent chapters will examine some of the possible reasons for this outcome but it seems that there are factors which stem from the nature of the social work task in the local authority services and from the roles and caseload responsibilities that fall to different designations, and which introduce constraints into the situation. These perhaps inhibit rather than encourage the kinds of development that were at one time envisaged.

SUMMARY

Most social workers in the local authority social services are using volunteers for two main types of activity—befriending and practical services, mainly for clients who are physically handicapped or elderly. They are less likely to use volunteers for work requiring special skills, counselling, group or community activities. In the probation service, however, volunteers are used more often on befriending and counselling than on practical types of service.

Three main reasons were offered by social workers and probation officers for using volunteers in the ways described: first, the personal and practical benefits to clients, probation officers being more likely to stress the personal than the practical; secondly, the nature of voluntary help as a special resource in itself—the something different and extra; and thirdly, the benefits to social workers themselves through the saving of their time, thus releasing them for what are judged to be more complex tasks.

Social workers' contact with their volunteers during the stages of enlisting their help varies according to the type of relationships social workers have with them. Considerably more social workers whose volunteers work under their direct guidance were involved with them at all stages. Indirect relationships, however, do not exclude some personal contact between social worker and volunteer, particularly at the stage of explaining what needs to be done. Even so, in the sample of users as a whole, substantial numbers of volunteers have no personal contact at any stage with the social workers themselves.

In the probation service most staff personally explain the task and supervise their volunteers.

NOTES

1 See, for instance, the group of studies listed in Note 1, Chapter 4.
2 In particular those of the National Institute for Social Work Research Unit, the Camden Social Services Department and the Croydon Social Services Department.
3 For the purposes of this study elderly people are those with no specific handicap, and physically handicapped people (unless otherwise stated) do not include those with difficulties of sight or hearing.
4 Some discrepancies may have arisen as a result of the fact that the respondents' descriptions of activities undertaken by volunteers in specific instances were coded by the researchers, whereas the more general picture was based on the respondents' pre-coded replies. It is possible that respondents may have emphasised a different aspect of the same type of activity from the researchers and *vice versa*.

5 See Note 1 Chapter 4.
6 It should again be emphasised that the limitations of the postal questionnaire method of collecting data necessarily prevented any detailed exploration of a qualitative nature of volunteers' activities and their collaboration with social workers. For the purposes of the present inquiry, only certain features of the deployment of voluntary workers in the statutory services could be noted. To take account of specific projects, of the subtle differences in the ways similar types of activities are carried out, or of their deeper meaning for all those concerned, would require close and more direct observation and study.

6 Volunteer Organisers

INTRODUCTION

The Aves Committee strongly recommended the appointment of full-time organisers of the work of volunteers in every service in which they were employed, and urged the local authority services, among others, to give more attention than hitherto to the organisation of voluntary work. Since that time, it has become increasingly the view that the appointment of specialist staff to recruit and select volunteers, so as to ensure their proper deployment and support them in their work, is a necessary step in the development of voluntary activity in the local authority services and in other services. Indeed, as will be seen, many such appointments have been made in recent years and were, according to the Volunteer Centre Survey (June, 1976) and also to the Centre's Directory (December, 1976), to be found in a substantial number of social services departments in England and Wales at the time of their inquiries.

Though cautious in the importance he assigns to their role, Darvill (1975), in an earlier review of voluntary involvement in social services departments, nevertheless includes the 'appointment of staff to specialise in the voluntary programme' as one measure necessary to the furtherance of such programmes. A small study of volunteer use in one probation area (Reading, 1976) also 'revealed the importance of having a person appointed as a co-ordinator'.

It was clearly, therefore, of interest in the present inquiry to try to discover from area offices in the sample the extent to which such appointments had been made or such specialist duties delegated, and to assess, where possible, the influence of such measures on the incidence of volunteer use and on the organisation of volunteers where their services were used. Additional data were obtained on the selection and training of volunteers, and the findings are described in Appendix IV.

The data collected on these lines do not cover the full sample, since only just over one-half of the area offices circulated completed the relevant questionnaires. Nevertheless, the results are of some interest, not least because they tend to confirm some of the findings of other studies, particularly the considerable differences in policy and practice among local authority social services departments concerning volunteers.

RESPONSIBILITY FOR VOLUNTEER ORGANISATION

Area officers were first asked whether there was a member of staff, at area or central office level or at both, with special responsibilities for volunteers.[1] The replies showed that in the majority of instances there were such specialist appointments, following three distinctive directions. The first and the most common was at area office level only; the second was at central office level only; the third was at both levels (Table 6.1). This meant that just under one-half of the area offices included in the inquiry could, if need be, call upon a special member of staff at headquarters—in a substantial number of cases in addition to their own.

Table 6.1   *Appointment of specialist staff for the organisation of volunteers: local authority area offices*

Appointment at	Number of offices
Area offices only[1]	35
Central office only	28
Central and area offices[1]	22
No appointment[1]	26
TOTAL[2]	111

[1]   Since it is possible that area officers replying to the supplementary questions may not have known about appointments in offices other than their own, these numbers may be lower than is in fact the case.

[2]   Excluding no replies and don't knows.

Not all such appointments were as volunteer co-ordinators, community liaison officers, voluntary help organisers or the like. Though these accounted for most of the specified replies, it was almost as frequent at area office level to find a social worker in a senior or management post who carried special responsibility for volunteers.

It was not clear from the data in what ways the role of the centrally-based members of staff differed from that of the locally-based. Certainly, from the information gathered in the exploratory phase of this study, and according to other evidence, there is considerable diversity from authority to authority in the functions of such appointments (see e.g. Davies and Filson, 1973; and Aves, 1976). These studies have shown that the main concern may be with community development, with the co-ordination of voluntary agencies, or with acting as a clearing house for volunteers. Even where specialist staff act in this latter role, however, they do so under a variety of titles, and are not necessarily wholly responsible for the recruitment, selection, training, allocation or supervision of volunteers, sharing these functions with others, or being responsible for only some of them.

Our data also suggest that the functions of specialist appointments in the supplement sample were very diverse, as were their titles. We were not able to pursue the question, however, of how far the functions and responsibilities of the individuals specified varied according to their titles, nor whether their titles represented similar duties from one authority to another or even from one area office to another.

Though it is not possible on the basis of the data obtained to assess precisely the scale of such appointments, our findings indicate first, that there may be relatively few local authorities in England and Wales without such specialist workers, whatever their title; and secondly, that such appointments, particularly with the title of volunteer organiser, voluntary service liaison officer or the like, and carrying special responsibility for volunteers, may well number over 500. This estimate, while approximate, is fairly consistent with that of the Volunteer Centre Survey (June, 1976). Our findings also suggest that the likelihood of there being someone with special responsibilities for volunteers at area office level is probably greater, the larger the number of social work staff in the area office.[2]

The Incidence and Scale of Volunteer Use in Area Offices
The incidence of volunteer use is not, apparently, much affected by the appointment or otherwise of an individual with special responsibilities for volunteers, and there were only marginal differences according to the nature of the appointment, or whether the appointment was at central or area office level. However, volunteer organisers or the like were associated with a rather higher incidence of indirect relationships between social workers and volunteers.[3] This may reflect the role of such organisers as 'go-betweens' and supporters for volunteers and professionals alike. It seems that in the probation service, where the direct relationship with volunteers predominates, this 'go-between' role is not so evident (Clarke, 1976).

Analysis was also made of the proportions using volunteers among the total social work complement of area offices. We thought this would be an additional check on the possible influence of the kind of specialist appointments described here on the use of volunteers, not only among the social workers taking part in the inquiry but also among all the social work staff in the area offices covered by the sample. The analysis showed first, that area offices varied considerably in the extent to which their social work staff as a whole were involved with volunteers. Thus, at one extreme no staff at all were using volunteers, while at the other all were doing so; and in nearly one in three offices the majority were. Most typical, however, was minority staff involvement, though some of these minorities were substantial.

Secondly, it was evident that the appointment of a specialist officer, or the delegation of special duties to a member of staff, made very little difference to the proportions of total social work staff using volunteers. Indeed, our findings were curious, in that in two of the four offices where all the social work staff were using volunteers there was no kind of specialist appointment. There was, however, a specialist appointment in three of the eleven offices where, at the time of the inquiry, no volunteers at all were being used. This apparent anomaly may be partly due to fluctuations over time in the use of volunteers.

Patterns of Collaboration

As described in Chapter 5, social workers when working with volunteers are more likely to explain to them in person what has to be done than to make the initial approach or themselves to supervise them. It was obviously of interest to discover the part played in these different stages of collaboration by the specialist officer. It was assumed that where there was such an officer, he or she would be likely to play a prominent role, especially where volunteers were not working under the direct guidance of social workers.

The findings suggest that this is indeed so. In the majority of the offices where there was someone with special responsibility for volunteers, he or she took responsibility for the initial approach to them; and in almost all these the individual in question was a volunteer organiser or the equivalent. Similar tendencies applied during the process of explaining what has to be done and, to an even greater extent in supervising volunteer activities.

The function of such specialists, however, is clearly not to replace the social worker in any of these activities, since substantial proportions of social workers, as noted earlier, also explained to volunteers what has to be done, and to a lesser extent supervised them. These activities do not, of course, exclude other specialist responsibilities, though according to the Volunteer Centre survey of June 1976 volunteer organisers still have a limited range of working methods.

Whatever the range, however, there does seem to be a large element of sharing between social workers and the specialist staff, particularly after the initial approach to the volunteer has been made. Moreover, as the earlier data suggest, there may well be a third participant—the outside agency. It is evident that this too played a considerable part in the deployment of volunteers, even when there was a member of staff with volunteer responsibilities within the area office.

More relevant to the apparently insignificant influence of such appointments on the use of volunteers may be the fact that many of these appointments have occurred in recent years. According to the Volunteer Centre (June, 1976) more of these appointments have occurred in the last three to four years (since 1973) than previously (though the voluntary sector is also included in this estimate). Some of the individuals specified in the present inquiry may, therefore, have been relatively new to their jobs and have had no time to influence matters in any marked degree. It is possible too that some of them may have been affected by the conditions to which Richards (1977) and Aves (1976) draw attention. The majority of volunteer organisers, according to their evidence, have received only rudimentary training, if any. They are inclined to feel, it seems, a sense of isolation and of 'floating in organisational space' (Richards), as well as suffering a lack of recognition, 'conflicting claims and expectations from volunteers and professionals', and even 'downright hostility' (Aves). Moreover, it seems that the majority of social services departments have not yet thought out their policy regarding volunteers in the statutory services (Aves, 1976).

SUMMARY

The evidence suggests that the majority of social services departments delegate responsibility for volunteers to someone either at central or at area office level, and that the majority of these persons are specially appointed volunteer organisers, co-ordinators, community liaison workers and the like. Where such responsibility has been delegated, there would seem to be three patterns of organisation. In the first and more intensive type, delegated or appointed persons function in both central and area offices. The second is at area level only, where in just under half the offices there was someone with volunteer responsibilities. And the third is at central office level only.

At the time of the inquiry, there did not appear to be any very marked variation in the incidence of volunteer use according to these three different patterns. Only where a volunteer organiser as such has been appointed do there appear to be more social workers using volunteers, and then it is on the basis of more frequent indirect relationships with them. Where there is a member of staff with volunteer responsibilities, he or she is likely to play a major part in enlisting voluntary help, in explaining what has to be done and in supervising them, but not to the exclusion of the social worker.

NOTES

1 In this comparatively new field of volunteer organisation ambiguity in nomenclature presents quite a few problems for research. These ambiguities are highlighted in the various reports on volunteer organisations which have appeared since our fieldwork took place (e.g. Aves, 1976; Volunteer Centre, May 1976; Richards, 1977). In our postal investigation we tried to distinguish first, those appointments which carried the word volunteer (or voluntary) in their title and which were specified appointments. Even so, some confusion may have arisen if the function of the appointment in question was directed mainly to voluntary organisations rather than to individual volunteers. Secondly, we distinguished the area management and senior staff who specifically included responsibility for volunteer deployment among their duties; and thirdly, we distinguished other members of staff with similar responsibilities. Community workers or community liaison officers were grouped together with volunteer organisers and co-ordinators. Thus, the analysis covers both those who have been specially appointed and those to whom additional duties have been designated.

2 Area offices vary in the size of their social work staff complement, but only within a relatively small range. Thus, there are comparatively few containing more than thirty social work staff. More than one in three have fewer than fifteen, while two in five have between fifteen and twenty. The average size is just under twenty social work staff. This suggests that however large their departments as a whole, just over one-half of the social work population work in relatively small units, even when the non-social work staff are taken into account.

3 In the same way that a volunteer organiser within the office appears to be associated with a higher proportion of social workers using indirect volunteers, so the existence of a volunteer bureau, or its equivalent, in the local authority area would seem marginally to have some effect. Just over one-half of the sample of offices were in areas containing such an agency and it is a reasonable assumption that these bureaux were used as a source of volunteers, particularly by those social workers involved only indirectly with their volunteers.

7 For and Against

While voluntary work in the social services is generally held to be a good thing, misgivings are often expressed about the difficulties and problems that may arise. Accordingly, we sought information on how social workers using volunteers assessed their experiences, where they drew the boundaries between the respective functions of professional and volunteer, and what they felt were the advantages and disadvantages of working with volunteers.

EXPERIENCES ASSESSED

Respondents were first asked about the last occasion on which they had used a volunteer and the effect of doing so on their work with the client in question. In assessing the effect, the majority of social workers and probation officers felt that there had been positive gains, mainly for themselves but also for their clients. Of those who felt this way, as many as one-half referred to the reduction in their workload, due in their view to the help of volunteers (Table 7.1). As one social worker put it, 'the volunteer has reduced the number of visits that I have had to make. This has reduced the pressure on my time'.

Smaller proportions felt they had gained in other ways. Their understanding about the case in question had increased (this was more so among probation officers); services not otherwise available had been provided; and the volunteer had proved to be a useful link between the professional worker and the client.

About one-fifth of both local authority social workers and probation officers felt that there had been gains—mainly personal ones—for the client as a result of using voluntary help, one respondent pointing out that 'the voluntary worker's skill in personal relationships has greatly contributed to the client's aware-ness of his problems'.

A similar proportion of local authority staff (but fewer proba-tion officers), however, had quite contrary views, feeling that the voluntary help used in the last instance had made no difference to them in any way. A similar proportion were uncertain. All in all, therefore, there were substantial minorities, particularly in the local authority sample, for whom the most recent intervention of a volunteer had not, evidently, brought any notable gains.

The question of time is often brought up in discussions on

Table 7.1 *Nature of difference made by volunteer's help in the last instance*

Nature of difference	Local authority social workers (% of total)	Probation officers
For social worker		
work-load reduced	52	50
increase in understanding of the case	8	15
services given not otherwise available	7	5
For client		
personal benefit	28	35
practical benefits	8	5
Other		
useful link between client and social worker/ services	5	6
local community connection, other	1	4
No reply	12	9
TOTAL[1][2]	100	100
(number)	(382)	(98)

[1] Respondents who felt voluntary help had made a difference.
[2] Multiple replies.

volunteers. More of the social workers' time, it is said, may be involved than they feel they can give or is justified. Yet, when asked about the effect on their time of using voluntary help generally, most local authority social workers considered that their time had been saved. Again, one in five felt that voluntary help had made little difference either way, but very few indeed that working with volunteers had taken up more time than they would otherwise have spent. As will be seen, however, such views by no means detracted from the value of voluntary help in many social workers' eyes.

A much smaller proportion of probation officers than of local authority workers thought that their time had been saved by using volunteers, while higher proportions either felt voluntary help had made little or no difference, or that it had involved more of their time than if no voluntary help had been available. This pattern of response may well reflect the much higher incidence of direct relationships with volunteers among probation officers and the greater amount of time they probably spend with them.

In order to assess the extent to which social workers were still well disposed towards volunteers, even if using them took up more time, respondents were asked to comment on their replies. Nearly one in three did so, most of them favourably.

Some of the comments clearly reinforced the opinions of many of the social workers that, though volunteers had indeed saved their time, this was not the only gain. One medical social worker referred to the fact that in addition to the volunteers being time-savers for her, they had also 'made a valuable contribution by demonstrating to the client that the community is concerned for his welfare'. Other comments were in the nature of explanations as to why, though the volunteers took up more of their time, their use was still thought worthwhile. Thus, some social workers felt that it was not just a question of saving, or of taking more, time since, if it were not for voluntary help, the particular service in question would not have been given. As one respondent said, 'I would not have been able to spend this kind of time, so the task would not have been done'.

This relatively favourable view of the time factor seems to confound the argument of those who do not use volunteers because they feel that this may take up more of their time than they can spare. But opinions on the time saved or gained by using volunteers are very subjective, and may vary considerably according to circumstances. We were not able to investigate this. As will be seen, however, some variation is evident in social workers' views on the advantages and disadvantages of using volunteers. Those currently working with volunteers have more positive viewpoints on the time question than those who no longer do so. It is widely known, moreover, and confirmed in the present inquiry, that many social workers feel that they work under considerable time pressure. The line dividing what is feasible and worthwhile for them on one occasion from what is not feasible and a waste of their time on another is probably a great deal finer than is generally recognised.

UNFAVOURABLE OCCURRENCES

Nevertheless, things cannot always go well, and respondents were therefore asked about the incidence of any unfavourable occurrences that might have arisen for anyone—client, volunteer, social worker or any other person—from working with volunteers. The replies show that, while for the great majority of respondents (nearly three-quarters), nothing of this order had arisen, nearly twice as many probation officers as local authority social workers had experienced such occurrences. Where things had gone wrong, it was more often the clients in the local authority sample who had been upset, while in the probation officer sample it was the volunteers, though probation officers also made rather more frequent references to other people being affected, including themselves.

The upsets described were attributed in the main to some aspect of the volunteers' attitudes or behaviour, mostly their 'lack of skill', but also their 'unreliability'. Thus, for instance, one voluntary worker was said to have become 'too possessive over a youth under supervision', protecting the boy to such an extent that there was 'a complete breakdown'. Her reports to the social worker 'in no way resembled the truth of what she was doing'. Another volunteer was said to have reported on visits to elderly clients, when in fact no such visits had been made. In this instance, the social worker had been the most upset, partly feeling 'that it was her lack of supervision that was to blame'.

Some clients' attitudes and behaviour were also held to have contributed to unfavourable situations, either because they had apparently rejected the volunteers' services or manipulated the volunteers in some way. Proportionately more than twice as many probation officers as local authority social workers felt clients had been responsible for things going wrong, mainly because in their experience volunteers had been rejected by clients.

In the local authority sample, though the numbers involved are small, an analysis was made of the incidence of unfavourable occurrences according to the nature of the service undertaken and the person helped. This suggests that there were proportionately fewer upsets where clients were receiving the more intensive kind of personal support (which, it will be recalled, generally entailed closer supervision of the volunteer by the social worker) than where clients were being befriended. Upsets arising from this more intensive support were more often attributed to the volunteers' lack of skill than to any other factor. It was rather surprising to find, moreover, that the volunteer was more likely to have been the 'injured party' when working with elderly clients and to have been more frequently rejected when working with children.

None of these tendencies is very marked, yet they serve to illustrate that bringing volunteer and client together is perhaps a more delicate matter than is sometimes assumed, requiring the correct balance of all the elements that contribute to things going well. By and large, on the basis of the opinions of the respondents in the present inquiry, a workable equilibrium seems to have been achieved in most instances.

BOUNDARIES

One element in such an equilibrium may be the recognition—explicit or implicit—by all concerned of the boundaries which define their respective roles. The Aves Committee (1969) considered that, whilst in particular situations the functions of social workers and volunteers needed to be defined, in general such boundaries should remain flexible, allowing changes and new developments to evolve. It was obviously important in the present inquiry to discover the social workers' own views on where the boundaries lay. They were accordingly asked if there was any type of case or service that they would not ask their volunteers to undertake and, if so, what this would be. Their replies indicate that the majority of respondents—over three-fifths in both samples— would draw the line somewhere. About one in four, however, were not sure, and a smaller proportion evidently saw no boundaries at all.

In describing the types of case and activity which they thought were unsuitable for volunteers, most social workers, as Table 7.2 shows, felt the boundaries were defined by casework situations which called for a degree of skill, understanding and experience, which in their view most volunteers would not have. This was sometimes expressed in general terms as, for instance, by an area officer who thought that volunteers should not be used in any 'situation which involved more than "tea and sympathy"', or by a social worker who considered that 'only routine visiting or advice should be given'.

Table 7.2   *Types of cases considered unsuitable for volunteers*

Type of case	Local authority social workers	Probation officers
Casework generally	34	26
Psychological/personal difficulties	32	32
Where statutory requirements involved	17	16
Families with special problems	14	8
Where confidentiality involved	9	7
Suitability of case depends on volunteer	5	18
Where volunteer at risk	4	19
Other (including particular stages of casework)	9	5
TOTAL[1] [2]	100	100
(number)	(371)	(91)

[1] Only users who feel there are cases unsuitable for volunteers.
[2] Multiple replies.

More often, respondents specified the kinds of cases or situations they had in mind. These might relate to individuals or families with psychological difficulties where for example, 'the disturbed personality would be too difficult to handle'. Others related to situations where misjudgement or mishandling might lead to serious consequences for everyone. The unsuitability of volunteers for people who are dying was also mentioned, particularly by hospital social workers; senior staff were the most likely to refer to the unsuitability of casework, while social work assistants (probably because they are not so often involved in it) were the least likely to do so.

Cases where statutory obligations (supervision orders made under the 1969 Children and Young Persons Act for example) were vested in the social worker, were referred to most often as being unsuitable for volunteers by area management staff and seniors. It was the social work assistants, on the other hand, who were most inclined to regard matters of confidentiality as the dividing line. One respondent saw 'confidentiality' combined with the question of 'ultimate responsibility' as the 'main problem' for the use of volunteers. The one-to-one relationship between social worker and client was sometimes considered too delicate and vital to risk the intrusion of 'an outsider'.

Other social workers drew their boundaries with different considerations in mind. Some, for example, felt they would not ask volunteers to do anything that they themselves were not prepared to do. There was also the need to protect the volunteers from 'manipulation' or from unpleasant conditions; and there were stages in casework as this is commonly understood in social work practice, like 'the crisis stage' or when 'specific assessments' were being made, when it was thought wiser for volunteers not to be involved. Probation officers, more often than local authority social workers, emphasised the need to protect the volunteer. More of them also felt that all depended on the volunteer.

The evidence thus suggests that social workers generally favour the drawing of fairly well-defined boundaries between the respective functions of the professional and volunteer, and that they define these boundaries so as to distinguish those tasks for which professional training and qualifications are required. This would seem to confirm the view that casework is one of the main areas of controversy where the function of volunteers is concerned (Darvill, 1975). Most social workers in the present inquiry show clearly enough where they stand in relation to this. The majority do not believe, evidently, that the voluntary helper may be more 'therapeutic to the client than the paid professional' or that the benefits of casework are largely 'mythical' (Darvill).

In practice, however, the lines may not be as hard and fast as they appear, particularly as there are some social workers who, in refusing to specify any boundaries at all, presumably have open minds on the issue. We were not able to discover within the scope of the present inquiry how fixed or strongly-held social workers' attitudes are towards the place of the volunteer. Perhaps these attitudes are more flexible than is sometimes assumed. According to Darvill, the 'appropriate division of labour' between professionals and volunteers is still debatable and open to bargaining and negotiation. Given that actions speak louder than words, however, the dominant view in local authority services suggests that the bargain so far negotiated with most of the profession is of relatively limited scope. This may be partly owing to structural factors within the local authority services, as is discussed in Chapter 9, that introduce certain rigidities into the negotiations. It may also have something to do with the attempts within the profession to redefine the social work task and the uncertainties about the meaning of social work itself.

ADVANTAGES AND DISADVANTAGES

Finally, social workers in the two samples were asked, in the light of their experiences, to comment on the main advantages and disadvantages of using the services of volunteers for their clients. There were three reasons for posing this question. First, it gave respondents an opportunity to sum up their views; second, it provided a rough measure of the degree of consistency in their replies generally to the assessment questions; and third, it enabled some comparison to be made between the respective views of social workers who were working with volunteers and those who were not.

The Advantages

Many social workers from both services clearly felt that there were multiple gains arising from voluntary help, and referred in their replies to more than one advantage. Table 7.3 shows that four main types of viewpoint emerge, corresponding closely to the reasons given for using volunteers in the ways discussed earlier.

First, there were the advantages that stem from the very nature of voluntary work. The volunteer is seen as having more time to give and giving it freely, as well as providing something intrinsically different from, and additional to, the services of the professional. Probation officers gave special emphasis to this latter quality, and more than twice as many of them as of local authority workers commented on it.

Thus, one respondent felt that volunteers were able to provide 'the kind of help and support' that she, 'due to lack of time and an inescapable image', would never be able to provide alone. Another social worker commented on the voluntary worker being 'voluntary and a free agent' and 'far less official' than the social worker. This, in the opinion of a probation officer, meant that 'unofficial relationships' could be established, which were sometimes 'more

Table 7.3   *Advantages of using volunteers*

Advantages	Local authority social workers (% of total)	Probation officers
Intrinsic to voluntary help		
volunteer's gift of time and services	25	34
volunteer offers something different and extra	21	50
sub-total	46	84
Benefits for social worker		
saving of time	28	19
general benefit	14	13
Sub-total	42	32
Benefits for client		
personal	25	36
practical	11	9
sub-total	36	45
Other		
Extends resources	19	7
Social/community benefits	8	8
Other (including benefits for volunteers)	3	–
None	3	1
No reply	5	5
TOTAL[1]	100	100
(number)	(623)	(141)

[1] Multiple replies.

useful in cases having anti-authoritarian problems'. Other comments emphasised 'the natural and warm relationship' a volunteer offers to the client, which gives a feeling of 'normality' and of 'commitment' that few social workers have the time to impart.

Secondly, there were the advantages to the social workers and probation officers themselves. These were mostly expressed as a saving of their time, but also in terms of supplementing their role and giving them additional support—comments which again correspond with the reasons given for using voluntary help. Fewer probation officers than local authority social workers, however, saw the advantages of using volunteers in these terms, mainly because, as we have seen, they were far less inclined to feel that using volunteers was time-saving for them.

Thirdly, there were specific advantages for the clients, particularly in a personal sense, though these were more often mentioned by probation officers than by local authority social workers. In emphasising the benefits to clients, one social worker referred to 'the widening of the interests of handicapped persons' as a result of voluntary help; clients had been 'relieved from worrying too much' and the volunteers 'had brought friendship' to many people in need of it.

Fourthly, there was the feeling (though less often in the probation service) that using volunteers had extended resources in some way—either those of the social worker or of the social services generally. Proportionately more management and senior staff held this view. References were made to the way the service provided by the department had been extended, and to volunteers being able 'to provide more regular and reliable visits' than was possible for the social worker. Relatively few replies referred to any social benefits brought about by involving the community through voluntary help, such as an increase in self-help activities, or the breaking down of barriers between 'the helpers and the helped'. Even fewer commented on any other advantages, such as benefits to the volunteer. Hardly any respondents found that there were no advantages at all.

The Disadvantages

The most striking feature of the response to the question on disadvantages is that almost one-half of both samples felt that there were no disadvantages in using voluntary help, evidence in itself of what seems to be a generally favourable view among social workers and probation officers of their voluntary workers (Table 7.4).

Nevertheless, it is clear that working with volunteers is not without its problems. The most often cited (by nearly one in three of both samples) are the extra trouble, effort and work involved, as well as the time taken up in supervising volunteers and in keeping a check on how their clients are faring. One social worker complained, for example, that volunteers 'need so much encouragement and supervision that the phantasies of saving time are rarely met'. Other typical comments referred to 'little or no feedback', 'difficulties in liaising effectively with voluntary workers who are only available in the evening', and to the disadvantages of sharing clients and having more than one person involved in their problems. There were also references to the tendency of volunteers to act 'too independently', and to the problem of ambiguity over the respective roles of the professional and the volunteer. In the opinion of one probation officer there was need 'to guard against the volunteer taking over', and in the view of another, 'confusion about the aims of the work' was a 'perennial problem'. A social worker also commented on 'the

Table 7.4 *Disadvantages of using volunteers*

Disadvantages	Local authority social workers (% of total)	Probation officers
None	46	45
Volunteers said to		
be more trouble generally	13	21
take more time	12	9
provide no feedback	6	1
sub-total	31	31
Volunteers said to		
be unreliable, etc.	15	8
lack skill/experience, etc.	14	18
sub-total	29	26
Other (including professional questions, disadvantages for clients)	10	6
No reply	8	4
TOTAL[1]	100	100
(number)	(623)	(141)

[1] Multiple replies.

difficulty of sorting out roles', as well as of maintaining 'on-going contact and of working together'.

Almost as many respondents—especially those with the largest caseloads, but noticeably fewer probation officers—felt that the main disadvantages of voluntary help arose from the volunteers themselves, and referred to what they termed their 'lack of skill and experience', their 'unreliability' and 'lack of commitment', their 'tendency to be unrealistic' and so on. One commented, for example, on the volunteers' 'liability to gossip' so that 'the neighbours often know as much, if not more, about the client, than do the social workers'; another, on 'their wanting to do more than they are capable of, promising provisions which are impossible, mainly through lack of knowledge'.

There were relatively few references to disadvantages concerning specifically professional questions, to the issues of accountability and confidentiality, to the blurring of the boundaries between professional and volunteer, or to threats to the professional's role and identity as such (though one probation officer did confess to a fear of losing his client). This suggests that where difficulties in working with volunteers arise, they are far more likely to add to day-to-day work problems than to uncertainties, if any, about their professional status and role.

It is noteworthy that proportionately far more social work assistants than fieldworkers felt there were no disadvantages whatsoever in using volunteers, and far fewer of them, where they did see disadvantages, attributed these to the volunteers' lack of skills or to the problems their use was said to create for the social worker. This is, perhaps, because assistants, as we have seen, are less likely to be using volunteers for activities requiring special skills. By contrast, social workers in senior and management posts were less likely to feel that there were no disadvantages involved in using voluntary help, and more often referred to the increased problems for social workers and to difficulties of a professional nature that could arise.

On balance, however, the advantages seem substantially to outweigh the disadvantages. Moreover, as Table 7.5 shows, working with volunteers is far more often associated with the saving of time and a reduction in workload, than with the occurrence of unfavourable incidents. This balance, and that between favourable and unfavourable experiences, is related, however, to the present scale on which volunteers are used; to the nature of their deployment and to the types of relationship between the volunteers and the professionals which have evolved. A shift in emphasis in any of these respects might affect the balance, particularly in the local authority services. In the probation service, where the incidence of volunteer use is higher, where direct relationships with volunteers predominate, and where volunteers' activities tend towards the more personal tasks, things seem to go wrong more often. Moreover, fewer probation officers feel that voluntary help has saved their time and more of them refer, among the disadvantages, to the extra demands made upon their time and energies by using volunteers. While this does not invalidate the generally high regard of probation officers for their volunteers, it indicates, nevertheless, that more intensive use of volunteers in the local authority services would require a greater investment than at present of the social workers' time and effort, without necessarily bringing more direct or immediate gains for themselves, even though there may be some for their clients.

SUMMARY

Generally, social workers have a consistently favourable view of their experiences with volunteers, irrespective of the type of relationship they have with them. There were comparatively high proportions who felt that voluntary help in the last instance had positively helped in terms of the work on the case in question, who had no unfavourable experiences to recount and who considered that volunteers saved their time. In this last respect, fewer probation officers shared this view.

Table 7.5 *Consistency of favourable views on volunteers*

Proportions holding favourable views	Local authority social workers (% of total)	Probation officers
No unfavourable occurrences with volunteers	73	64
Volunteer's help in last instance made a difference to their workload, etc.	64	70
Voluntary help saves their time	69	49
No disadvantages in using volunteers	46	45
TOTAL (number)	(623)	(141)

Where difficulties did arise, it was usually because the volunteers were thought to lack the appropriate skills and, where there were disadvantages, these were mainly associated with these same deficiencies, or with the extra work that the use of volunteers was said to create for the social workers. Moreover, substantial minorities in both samples considered that there were no disadvantages in working with volunteers. Where there were, these on balance were outweighed by the advantages, prominent among which—particularly for the probation officers—were the intrinsic qualities of voluntary work itself, and the benefits such work brought to the social workers.

Nevertheless, most respondents favoured the drawing of boundaries that define the respective contributions of the professional and volunteer, and considered that there were situations, mainly involving casework, where the voluntary contribution was inappropriate and should not be given.

8 Not Working with Volunteers

INTRODUCTION

In the local authority services, social workers who are not working with volunteers are nearly as typical as those who are. This, as indicated in Chapter 4, is mainly due to the fact that substantial proportions of social workers stop using volunteers at some stage in their careers. Those in positions of seniority and management for example, are less likely than others to use volunteers, though they once did. This, so it seems, is mainly because their increased seniority is associated either with the giving up altogether of case-loads or with much smaller caseloads and with changes in their com-position. A similar tendency seems to apply to many of the more experienced and qualified fieldworkers who once used volunteers. Even if not yet promoted, these social workers are nevertheless distinguishable from others by their smaller and differently-composed caseloads. By contrast, social workers who have never used volunteers are not only relatively few, but also tend to be the newer recruits to social work.

From these two tendencies together, it looks as if working with volunteers may mark an intermediate stage in the career histories of social workers as they make their way through the social services hierarchy. As new entrants, they do not immediately use volunteers (though many of them will eventually), perhaps because of their preoccupations with establishing themselves in their new careers and adjusting to their new responsibilities. As the more qualified among them gain in experience, skill and seniority, and as their casework responsibilities change, so they stop using volunteers. Moreover, this discontinuity, unlike the temporary fluctuations in the use of volunteers resulting from the ebb and flow of clients in caseloads or of the supply of volunteers, is probably fairly perman-ent.

A rather different situation is evident in the probation service. Here the non-users are a smaller minority than in the local authority services but they, too, represent mainly former users. Unlike the local authority sample, however, the senior officers are only a little more likely than other probation staff to have discontinued using voluntary help. This is, perhaps, because a much higher proportion of them than of seniors in the local authority services retain their caseloads.

REASONS FOR NOT USING VOLUNTEERS

Though seniority, experience and casework responsibilities are important elements in the giving up of voluntary help, it was obviously important to question social workers themselves as to the reasons why they were not at the time using volunteers, and to discover whether there were any differences in viewpoint between those who had once used them and those who had never done so. Respondents were accordingly asked to state in their own words why they were not using volunteers in any way.

Broadly speaking, three main reasons were given why volunteers were not being used at the time of the inquiry (Table 8.1). The first and most important of these, for local authority social workers, related to factors which in one way or another were said to affect the supply or availability of volunteers, and included references to the lack of 'suitable' volunteers. The second related to factors associated with the size and composition of caseloads; and the third to respondents' feelings that neither their cases nor they themselves needed the services that volunteers could give. A rather different order of importance was revealed in probation officers' replies; here, it was the size and nature of their caseloads which took precedence.

Organisational difficulties were varied, and were commented on by just under two-fifths of the sample. They included the 'need', as expressed by one social worker, 'for a person or persons with a great deal of time to devote to recruiting, assessing and training volunteers'; the conditional 'ifs and buts' that met simple requests, making a social work assistant feel that it was often easier 'to do the job oneself'; and, for another social worker, the 'lack of a bank of volunteers' for her present area team. The question of responsibility for volunteer organisation was emphasised in more than one way by many respondents. Many of the comments implied that such matters as the recruitment, supply, and even supervision, of volunteers should be handled by specialist agencies or officers, rather than by the social workers themselves. A deputy area officer had 'serious reservations about the organisation of volunteers' in his area, based on the experience of volunteers being promised and 'nothing happening, in spite of reminders'. This suggests that, for him, changes were required in the existing organisational arrangements for the supply of volunteers. A similar view is implied by a fieldworker's statement that he did not use volunteers because his 'authority doesn't provide them'. Another fieldworker, on the other hand, attributed the 'insufficient time and thought put into the organisation of volunteers' mainly to 'the agency', but partly to himself. Some respondents also referred to proposed organisational changes in their offices, such as the appointment of a

Table 8.1 *Reasons for not using volunteers*

| Reasons | Local authority social workers | | | Probation officers |
	Not now using	Never have used	Total (% of total)	All non-users
Organisational				
lack of or poor organisation, etc.	19	17	18	12
volunteers/suitable volunteers not available	18	26	20	22
sub-total	37	43	38	34
Size and nature of caseload				
cases not appropriate	24	16	22	17
too few cases	11	5	9	30
sub-total	35	21	31	47
Clients/social workers do not need volunteers	21	22	21	15
Social workers too busy, not enough time, too difficult	7	8	7	7
Social worker's doubts, disapproval	5	16	8	2
Other (including client's attitude, new appointment)	8	10	8	8
No reply	15	8	13	5
TOTAL[1]	100	100	100	100
(number)	(404)	(176)	(580)	(60)

[1] Multiple replies.

volunteer organiser, hoping that this would improve the supply of volunteers. Such viewpoints, as we have seen earlier, are consistent with the tendency for local authority social workers to rely comparatively often on outside agencies or specialist staff for initiating and maintaining contact with volunteers.

There were also references to the difficulty—sometimes the 'extreme difficulty'—of obtaining volunteers or what were termed 'suitable' ones, particularly by social workers who had never used them and by those with the larger caseloads. It was not always easy to interpret this type of comment. It might reflect a local shortage of volunteers or mean that some social workers had special demands not easily matched by the volunteers who were available. There was also the possibility that such difficulties in the supply of volunteers made it easier for those reluctant to use volunteers not to do so. One probation officer was quite explicit about his reluctance in this respect, remarking that 'accredited volunteers selected are all middle-aged and upper middle-class', and therefore, in his view, 'unsuitable'.

The second main reason for not using volunteers was related to the composition and—particularly for former users and for probation officers generally—to the size of caseloads. Local authority social workers, however, were much more likely to feel that their caseloads were not appropriate ones to share with volunteers than to feel that they were too small, whereas the reverse tendency applied in the probation service.

Further analysis showed that in the local authority services, while those who felt that they had too few clients to need volunteers tended indeed to have smaller caseloads (under twenty cases), this was less often so for those who argued that their caseloads were not suitable for volunteers. This would correspond with one of the major findings of the present inquiry (discussed fully in Chapter 9), that it is the composition, rather than the size, of caseloads which is a major determinant of the use of volunteers in the local authority services. As will be seen, smaller caseloads are far less likely than larger ones to contain as many of the clients, if any, as are generally considered to be the most suitable recipients for voluntary help.

Probation officers, in their reasons for not using volunteers, more often referred to the smallness of their caseloads than to their composition. This suggests that here, factors other than caseload composition may influence volunteer use. But, presumably, caseloads in the probation service are no less 'complex' than many of those which in the local authority services were felt to need exclusive professional skills and which, for that reason, were considered as unsuitable for volunteers.

The third main reason for not using volunteers was that social workers thought their clients did not need voluntary help or would not benefit from it, or that they themselves did not need to call upon voluntary services. Some of the more cryptic references to there being 'no need' for volunteers might, if more fully explored, have indicated a reluctance to use them. Many social workers, however, explained their reasons more fully.

They felt that there was adequate provision and support for their clients in the community, such as the social work assistant who thought that there was a 'good community neighbourly spirit in the locality' so that the need for volunteers was 'kept to a minimum'. Others, particularly social work assistants (and also trainees), commented on the fact that specific services associated with volunteers, like escorting or transport, were not needed at the time.

Other reasons for not using volunteers were offered by comparatively few social workers. There was the feeling that there was not enough time and energy to spend on working with volunteers, or that the volunteer gave an 'added dimension to cases, and thus required more rather than less work'. Others—mainly fieldworkers—referred to doubts about using voluntary help or the difficulties of doing so, though hardly any probation officers had such reservations. Sometimes it seemed as if a single experience—as, for instance, where one volunteer had 'failed to do any work whatsoever on the case allocated to her'—had given rise to a continuing resistance. But more often the references were less specific, volunteers being referred to as 'unreliable'; or as unable, in the words of one social work assistant, 'to sustain effort and interest once the novelty has worn off'. The problem of 'geographical distance' in a large rural area was also mentioned. The fear of overinvolvement on the part of volunteers was shared by a number of respondents, expressed particularly sharply by a probation officer who wrote of the dangers of voluntary workers 'acting out their own fears, anxieties and frustrations—to the client's detriment'. A few respondents, particularly those who had never used volunteers, attributed their own non-use to the policies or practice of their departments or colleagues; to clients themselves who did not like the idea of voluntary help; to the temporary nature of their present situation (this applied particularly to the probation officers), or to their lack of experience, especially where they were new to their jobs.

There is very little expression of explicit disapproval of the idea of using the services of volunteers or of hostility generally, though it is possible that underlying some of the doubts and uncertainties are irrational fears, such as the possible loss of professional status or the criticism of professional methods as a result of involving volunteers. Most of the reasons advanced for not using volunteers would seem, however, to have a rational basis. Nevertheless, substantial proportions in both samples evidently consider that because of the size and composition of their caseloads, and the circumstances of their casework, volunteers are inappropriate and unnecessary.

This suggests that even if a higher scale of volunteer use were made possible by overcoming the difficulties of organisation to which some non-use is attributed, there are still likely to be instances where, in the judgement of the social workers concerned, there is no place for the volunteer.

BOUNDARIES

We were concerned to discover from the non-users something of their views about the place of the volunteer, and to trace any differences there might be as between those who had once used volunteers and those who had never done so. We were also curious as to whether the non-users differed in any significant way from those currently using volunteers in their definition of the respective roles of professionals and volunteers. Non-users were asked, therefore, in a pre-coded question, to indicate first, which of the four main types of service—practical tasks, work requiring special skills or knowledge, befriending, and counselling—volunteers in their opinion could or should not do; and secondly, which of the client groups they considered volunteers could or should not help. They were also given the opportunity to indicate if they had no opinion either way.

Activities

Virtually all non-users agreed on the suitability of practical activities, and almost as many on the suitability of a befriending type of service. Fewer, but still the majority, considered work requiring special skills to be suitable, but only a minority approved of counselling as an activity for volunteers.

Indeed, the idea that volunteers might become involved in counselling is clearly not a popular one, evoking more disapproval than uncertainty particularly among probation officers. Rather more of them, however, than of local authority social workers positively favoured the idea. They were also more inclined to feel that volunteers could provide services requiring special skills.

For local authority social workers and probation officers alike, it would seem that the simpler and the more straightforward the task, and the further removed it is from casework, the more likely it is to be regarded as suitable for the volunteer.

Those who have used voluntary help but no longer do so are more likely to find it suitable at each level of activity. This—for seniors and the more experienced fieldworkers especially—is particularly marked with counselling activities. Former users would thus seem to be rather more inclined than those with no experience at all to extend the boundaries of volunteer activity—at least in principle —and thus widen their general scope.

Clients

Non-users—in the same way as users—also consider that it is more appropriate for volunteers to help some client groups than others. Elderly people, and those who suffer from deafness, blindness or other types of physical handicap, come highest in their rank order.[1]

Almost as high are the physically ill or those who have mental handicaps. Next are children, prisoners and their families, followed by those with mental illnesses of different kinds, those who are homeless or who, as individuals or families face a variety of problems. The lowest in rank order are adults and children whose circumstances bring them before the courts, and cases of fostering or adoption. Moreover, where children are concerned, uncertain attitudes are expressed as often as disapproving ones, suggesting that in this instance many social workers have not yet made up their minds either way.

The respective ranking orders of former users of volunteers and of those who have never used them are virtually identical. In every instance proportionately more former users consider the client groups in question could be helped by volunteers, the difference growing larger as the position of each client group in the ranking order falls. Only in cases of fostering and adoption do the differences between the two groups disappear.

The experience of having worked with volunteers would thus seem to do little more, in terms of extending the scope of voluntary activity, than reinforce certain patterns of thinking which are only a little less prevalent among those without such experience. It does not radically change the pattern itself which, as we have seen, is shared to a relatively high degree by the current users of volunteers. Moreover, non-users, too, have virtually the same order of preferences regarding the client groups with whom they would most like to work if given the choice—namely children and families. These clients, however, particularly the children before the courts or being fostered or adopted, are the least likely to be considered as suitable for voluntary intervention. The less preferred clients, on the other hand, such as elderly or physically handicapped people, are the most likely to be considered as suitable recipients of voluntary help.[2]

Users and non-users alike, therefore, clearly favour the drawing of boundaries which define the respective roles of social workers and volunteers, and would seem to apply the same criteria for doing so. In other words, non-users, too, are mainly on the side of those who argue that casework situations require professional intervention—sometimes to the exclusion of the volunteer—and favour a division of labour, in which the volunteers' activities follow fairly conventional patterns.

It is possible that one of the factors influencing this approach is the tendency for the more senior, experienced and qualified social workers (who, for that reason, exercise an important influence on social work practice) to be the least likely to use volunteers themselves. Their frame of reference for the relative functions of volunteers and professionals, rather than belonging to the here and now, may stem from a past when their caseloads were probably larger and less specialised, and included elderly and physically handicapped clients who, as we have seen, are the most likely recipients of voluntary help. This past predates, as it were, what is handed on and, if anything, may serve to perpetuate conventional or stereotyped attitudes regarding the scope for voluntary activity and the intervention of the volunteer.

Any new developments in the use of voluntary help would thus seem to be dependent on the least, rather than the more, skilled and experienced social worker. Some might argue that there are advantages in diminishing the influence of the professionally qualified on the voluntary sphere. Nevertheless, the less experienced and qualified the social workers, the more likely they are to have caseloads which, by their size and composition, lead them to use volunteers in more set ways. These findings seem to highlight a quandary for the social work profession. Though the profession accepts, in principle, that volunteers have a place in the social services, it is nevertheless apprehensive in practice about their suitability for the various tasks that need to be done, except by and large in somewhat restricted terms.

ADVANTAGES AND DISADVANTAGES

To round off the picture, social workers not working with volunteers were also asked to give their views on the main advantages and disadvantages of voluntary help. We were interested in comparing their views with those of the social workers currently involved with volunteers. We were also interested in looking at the differences between the opinions of the former users who could, of course, draw on their past experience, and of those without any experience of voluntary help whose opinions were presumably shaped by other influences.

The Advantages

The Local Authority Sample. There are, in fact, some interesting differences between the two groups of non-users in what they saw as the main advantages of using volunteers. The most marked is in the much higher proportion of former users, compared to the 'nevers', who referred to the special contribution that voluntary help, by its intrinsic nature, provides (Table 8.2). Roughly equivalent proportions in both groups commented on the advantages of voluntary help to social workers (both generally and in relation to the saving of their time), and on the social benefits—the increase in community involvement and the like. Rather fewer of those who have never worked with volunteers commented on the personal benefits to clients, however, or on the extension of resources available to clients through voluntary help. And perhaps it is significant that proportionately rather more of them than of former users, felt that there were no advantages at all in using volunteers.

Thus, for the former users of volunteers the inherent qualities of

Table 8.2   *Advantages of using volunteers: non-users*

| Advantages | Local authority social workers | | | Probation officers |
	Not now using	Never have used	Total (% of total)	All non-users
Intrinsic to voluntary help				
Volunteer's gift of time and service	30	21	26	42
Volunteer offers something different and extra	30	19	26	42
sub-total	60	40	52	84
Benefits for social worker				
General benefit	20	21	17	17
Saving of time	16	18	18	12
sub-total	36	39	35	29
Benefits for client				
personal	20	13	17	17
practical	12	13	12	10
sub-total	32	26	29	27
Other				
extends resources	21	9	17	5
social/community benefits	17	12	15	13
Other (including benefits for volunteers)	1	2	1	–
None	5	15	8	5
No reply	3	9	5	1
TOTAL[1]	100	100	100	100
(number)	(404)	(176)	(580)	(60)

[1] Multiple replies.

voluntary help far exceed any other advantages it may bring, the benefits for the social workers and for the client being more or less evenly balanced. For those who have never used volunteers, however, these inherent qualities of voluntary effort and the benefits that using volunteers brings to social workers are more or less of equal emphasis. Of less importance for them, evidently, are the benefits that working with volunteers may produce for clients. These differences would suggest that changes in the way volunteers are perceived come with the experience of working with them, rather than as a result of other influences.

The Probation Sample. Probation officers, most of whom, as we have seen, are former users of volunteers, tended to give the same order of emphasis to the various advantages of using volunteers as those who formerly used volunteers in the local authority sample. A far higher proportion of non-users in the probation service, however, gave precedence to the unique role and contribution of the volunteer as, indeed, did their colleagues among the users of volunteers.

The Disadvantages

The Local Authority Sample. When referring to the advantages of using volunteers, those who had formerly worked with them generally tended to have a more favourable view of them than those who had not. For the disadvantages, it can be seen from Table 8.3 that a rather different picture emerges. Those who at one time worked with volunteers tend, if anything, to view them less favourably than those who have never done so.

First, compared with social workers who had never become involved with volunteers, former users made far more frequent references to what they described as the unreliability, lack of commitment, overidentification and other similar shortcomings of volunteers, as well as to their reported lack of skill and experience.

Secondly, those who no longer worked with volunteers, particularly if they were in management or senior posts, were more likely than those who had no experience of them to emphasise the trouble, work and effort—the need for 'regular, frequent and often intensive support'—that arose for the social worker, and the exra time involved. Finally, rather fewer of the former users felt there were no disadvantages.

The Probation Sample. The non-users among the probation officers, while far less often critical of volunteers as such, were almost as likely as the former users in the local authority sample to comment on the problems that arose for the professional when

Table 8.3   *Disadvantages of using volunteers: non-users*

Disadvantages	Local authority social workers			Probation officers
	Not now using	Never have used	Total	All non-users
			(% of total)	
Volunteers said to be unreliable	34	19	29	15
lack skill/ experience, etc.	30	22	28	22
sub-total	64	41	57	37
Volunteers said to be more trouble generally	25	13	21	22
take more time	7	13	7	15
provide no feedback	10	10	10	10
Professional questions (including boundaries, confidentiality, accountability)	10	13	11	5
Other (including disadvantages to client)	9	9	9	–
None	18	26	20	27
No reply	4	12	7	–
TOTAL[1]	100	100	100	100
(number)	(404)	(176)	(580)	(60)

[1] Multiple replies.

using volunteers. On the other hand, a rather higher proportion of them felt there were no disadvantages at all.

The evidence suggests, therefore, that while the experience of having worked with volunteers tends to enhance the social workers' view of voluntary workers' inherent qualities, it also tends to accentuate in their eyes the drawbacks of voluntary effort. This, however, rarely manifests itself as active disapproval of the principle of volunteer use. Moreover, as with the users of volunteers, on balance, the advantages of working with them outweigh the disadvantages, though by a much narrower margin than for the current users.

INCONGRUITIES

This tendency among former users of volunteers to stress the intrinsic quality of voluntary help, while at the same time emphasising the volunteers' shortcomings, is brought sharply into relief when their opinions on the advantages and disadvantages of using volunteers are compared with those of social workers who are currently involved with voluntary workers. Amongst local authority social workers this comparison shows first, that it is the former users who emphasise, above all, the intrinsic contribution of voluntary workers. Secondly, when opinions on the disadvantages of using volunteers are compared, the former users of volunteers, and particularly the seniors among them, are far more likely than current users to be critical of what they feel are the volunteers' shortcomings and (though the differences are less marked) to refer to the extra work and effort that volunteers create for the social worker. Moreover, relatively few of them, compared with current users, feel there are no disadvantages at all.

In the probation service, these tendencies are not so marked but still evident. Users and non-users alike place greatest emphasis on the special role of the voluntary worker, but larger proportions of current users than of non-users refer to the personal benefits to clients deriving from voluntary help.

Yet, non-users in the probation service (most of whom once worked with volunteers) are, as are their counterparts in the local authority services, no more likely than users to comment on the problems that arise for social workers, particularly those associated with collaboration between professional and volunteer, with the sharing of cases with volunteers or with keeping in touch with what is happening. They are, however, more likely to raise the questions of unreliability and lack of skills. They also less often feel that there are no disadvantages, compared with those probation officers who are actually using voluntary help.

Thus, in both samples, those who have formerly worked with volunteers perceive them in very different terms from those who are currently involved, or have never been so. First, they are much more likely to subscribe to a concept of voluntary help where the volunteers' freedom of choice to give their services is the essential element. In other words, they tend to emphasise the underlying principle which sustains beliefs in the value of voluntary service. Secondly, they nevertheless tend to have a less favourable view of volunteers in practice, commenting more often than others on their various demerits, and on the problems arising for the social worker.

These are apparently incongruent standpoints. They are not accounted for by the attitudes of social workers who stop working with volunteers as they move into more senior posts, for these are only a minority among former users of volunteers. Indeed, it may be assumed that these social workers would feel more responsibility for maintaining standards of social work practice, and consequently lend their support to the principle of voluntary service. They may be more critical, however, than other workers when voluntary work fails to meet their expectations.

It is possible, of course, that former users of volunteers may be more representative of social workers whose experiences of voluntary help have been less satisfactory than has so far proved to be the case for the current users, perhaps as a result of differences in their caseloads. Some former users may have been more ambitious in their use of volunteers and have given more time than they now feel they can spare. Either of these experiences may have led a user to give up volunteers. Yet adverse criticism of volunteers, or references to the problems they apparently create for social workers, were rarely offered as reasons for having given up working with volunteers. Perhaps by default, social workers who felt the most strongly about the principle, but who were the least 'successful' in practice, still thought that other reasons for not working with volunteers took greater precedence.

It is also possible that former users, who are likely to have had longer than average experience in social work, may have used the services of volunteers for longer than average, and may have stopped using them because they feel they have done their stint, or because they have evolved a method of working which is easier without volunteers—particularly as the nature of their caseload changes. Perhaps their support for the principle of voluntary help is not necessarily diminished, but the disadvantages are no longer offset by the gains. Or perhaps having passed through the initial and intermediate stages of their careers, and having become established, they are—as is expected of them—merely upholding the conventional wisdom of the profession.

SUMMARY

The majority of non-users have once used volunteers but no longer do so. This is mainly due to the tendency for casework and capabilities to change in the local authority services as social workers gain experience and assume senior positions. Social workers without any experience at all of using voluntary help are relatively few—particularly in the probation service—and represent more of the newer recruits to the profession.

The reasons for not using volunteers rarely include any explicit disapproval of doing so. Where volunteers are not used, therefore, it is said to be mainly due to factors that influence the supply and organisation of volunteers, to some change in the social workers' status and caseload or both, and to their feelings that volunteers are not needed in their present circumstances.

The perspectives of the non-users on the place of the volunteer appear to be no broader, on the whole, than those of the current users. A common frame of reference evidently operates, based on the view that the simpler and more straightforward the task, and the further removed from casework, the more likely it is to be regarded as suitable for the volunteer. Furthermore, the experience of working with volunteers seems to do little more, in terms of extending the scope of voluntary activities, than reinforce views which are only a little less prevalent among those without any experience at all of working with volunteers.

Commenting on the advantages and disadvantages of using volunteers, former users made more frequent references than those without any experience to the volunteer's special contribution. Thus, they seemed to subscribe more strongly than others to the principle of working with volunteers. Nevertheless, it is they who, more often than others, see disadvantages in using volunteers, particularly because of what they describe as the volunteers' own shortcomings.

NOTES

1 The client groups were ranked according to differences in the proportions of social workers' views as to their suitability for the involvement of volunteers.
2 Only a one-to-one comparison would show the actual degree of correspondence between social workers' preferences and their views as to which client groups should be helped.

PART THREE   THE SOCIAL WORK TASK AND THE USE OF VOLUNTEERS

9 Caseloads–
the Determining Factor

INTRODUCTION

The reorganisation of the statutory services in Scotland in 1969, and in England and Wales two years later, implemented the recommendations of the Kilbrandon and Seebohm Committees (1964 and 1968) for a unified approach to a range of social needs. These had been previously served by specialised social work skills and by separate administrations. These divisions, in the Committees' view, led to deficiencies in the nature and the quality of the service provided.

The tasks of social workers were accordingly redefined within the new structure, and social work practice changed in consequence. There was a significant shift from the specialised to the mixed caseload. Moreover, with the new obligations of the statutory agencies the former emphasis in social work on a psychotherapeutic method of approach has given way to more practical forms of help and to what is described as the relief function (Leonard, 1973; Smith and Harris, 1972). Since reorganisation, virtually all field-workers have been expected and, if qualified, trained to work with a variety of clients and types of problem, and to use a variety of social work methods.

Underlying the present inquiry, therefore, was the assumption that caseloads of most social workers would include among their clients elderly and handicapped people, who we have seen to be generally regarded as the most suitable recipients of voluntary help. There was also the fact that the general duties of social workers in local authority area offices would include where necessary the mobilisation of resources, of which volunteers might be part (Cogan and Terry, 1971).

Yet the pilot study had shown that mixed caseloads and a combination of social work methods did not necessarily mean that the social workers concerned were using the services of volunteers. This seemed to be due partly to the considerable variation in the degree of mix in caseloads and in the size of the caseloads themselves. The evidence of the pilot study suggested that some specialisation in relation to clients has continued to exist in the local authority services, if only in the sense that in some caseloads certain types of social need or client group predominate, sometimes to the virtual exclusion of any other. It was also evident that some social workers more than others were preoccupied with one type of social work intervention rather than with several. Thus, while the unitary or generic approach in social work practice is the most prevalent in local authority social services departments, there are some deviations from this.

It was clearly important, therefore, that the present inquiry should provide data on the caseloads and methods of work of social workers. We wanted to discover the extent to which variations in the size and composition of caseloads, and in the type of social work attention given, were associated, if at all, with variations in the deployment of volunteers and in the patterns of relationships established with them. Recognising that the size of caseloads was, on its own, an inadequate and perhaps misleading measure of caseload activity, or of the nature of the work demands, questions were devised which we hoped would indicate the composition of caseloads, the type of social work activity that was undertaken, and the time spent in these activities.

The purely factual aspects of caseloads, however, needed to be considered in the light of the attitudes and opinions of social workers about the work they do. The questioning was extended, therefore, so that the information collected would cover, as in the Southampton studies carried out by June Neill and colleagues (Neill *et al.*, 1973 and 1976), any preferences of social workers for particular client groups or social work methods, and their assessments of the pressures and stresses in their working lives. As a result, it has been possible to explore the links between their attitudes and opinions about these matters and their current workloads on the one hand and their use of volunteers on the other.

This chapter describes the findings of the present inquiry on these questions. Probation officers and hospital-based social workers are excluded from the analysis because of their more specialised caseloads.

CASELOAD SIZE

Social workers were asked to give as accurately as possible the number of clients making up their current caseloads, and the number of clients represented in each client group, according to the predefined categories listed in the questionnaire.[1] The accuracy of the figures given could not be verified. Moreover, recording systems vary, so that the term 'current caseload' may have had somewhat different meanings in different area offices. Checks, however, were made on the consistency of the figures given and comparisons made with other studies. These seemed satisfactory enough but some margin of error must be accepted.

As was mentioned earlier, local authority social workers tend, as might be expected, to relinquish or reduce their caseloads as they move into senior and management posts. Thus, while for the sample as a whole just over one in eight did not carry caseloads at the time of the inquiry, it was evident that this proportion was largely accounted for by area managers and senior social workers of whom only one-third and two-thirds, respectively, had caseloads at the time of the inquiry (Table 9.1). The proportion of social workers using the services of volunteers was naturally far higher among those who were carrying caseloads than among those who were not. Thus, one factor which would appear to depress the incidence, if not the scale, of voluntary help in the local authority services, is the relative absence of caseloads among the more senior grades. As we saw earlier, however, when senior staff do have caseloads, volunteers are used by almost as high a proportion of them as by social workers of other designations, except for social work assistants of whom a much higher proportion work with volunteers.

Table 9.1   *Designation and caseloads: local authority social workers*[1]

	Area officers/ deputies	Senior social workers	Field workers	Trainees	Social work assistants	Total
			(% of total)			
Proportion with caseloads	32	68	96	94	87	85
TOTAL[2]	100	100	100	100	100	100
(number)	(96)	(160)	(610)	(65)	(121)	(1,052)

[1]   This and all subsequent tables in this chapter and in Appendix VI exclude hospital-based social workers.
[2]   Excluding no replies.

Some social workers without caseloads nevertheless did draw upon voluntary help. This is not so inconsistent as it seems. Many of those concerned, particularly in management and senior posts, had apparently become involved in enlisting the help of volunteers for clients who, while not strictly their own, had been assessed by them as requiring voluntary help. Some social work assistants without caseloads had similarly contacted volunteers for clients whom they had visited, but for whom they had no direct on-going responsibility.

For those carrying caseloads, however, this study confirms other research findings—notably, the Southampton 1973 and 1976 studies—regarding the considerable variation in the size of case-loads carried by social workers in the local authority services.[2] These variations, though to a limited extent affected by the presence of part-time workers, seem to be more strongly influenced by the smaller average caseload size (averaging 20 cases) of seniors and management staff. Larger caseloads—between 40 and 100 cases—are found mainly among fieldworkers and social work assistants, considerably more of the latter carrying the largest caseloads of all—100 cases or more. The distribution of caseload size among fieldworkers follows, interestingly enough, the shape of a more or less normal curve, whereas for other designations, the shape of the distribution curve is skewed. (Figure 9.1). Trainees, as might have been expected, tend to have smaller caseloads than fieldworkers and social work assistants though as many as one in ten, at the time of the inquiry, were carrying more than 60 cases.

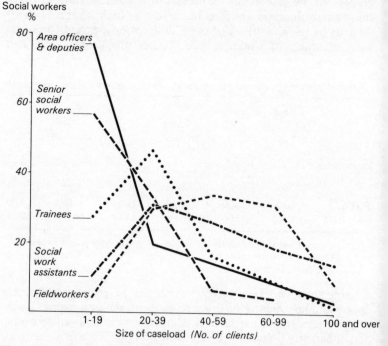

Figure 9.1   *Caseload size and designation: local authority social workers*

Thus the average caseload for fieldworkers (52) is somewhat higher in the local authority services than for their equivalents in the probation service—just under 40 (Cmnd 6590, 1976)—but lower (57) than that in the Southampton study (Neill *et al.*, 1976). Caseload sizes were on average higher for unqualified than for qualified staff, and this was as much due to the higher caseloads of unqualified fieldworkers as of social work assistants. There were only marginal differences in caseload size, however, according to length of experience, but a distinctive tendency for the number of cases carried to increase with age, so that the over-55s on average carry the largest caseloads of all and the under-35s the smallest.

As caseloads increase in size, however, so do the proportions of social workers using volunteers, even when allowance is made for the influence of designation by excluding all but fieldworkers from the analysis. This tendency is particularly marked among those with caseloads of more than 60 cases, among whom nearly two-thirds use volunteers, compared with fewer than one-half who do so among those with under 40 cases. Moreover, the higher the number of cases carried, the greater, proportionately, the number of fieldworkers who work directly with all or some of their volunteers. (Table 9.2).[3]

Table 9.2   *Size of caseload and use of volunteers; local authority social workers: fieldworkers only*

Type of relationship	Size of caseload		
	Under·40	40 - 59 (% of total)	Over 60
Users volunteers under social workers' guidance			
indirect	32	34	36
indirect and direct	11	14	20
direct	5	4	8
sub-total	48	52	64
Non-users not now using volunteers	34	30	23
never have used volunteers	18	18	13
sub-total	52	48	36
TOTAL[1]	100	100	100
(number)	(184)	(194)	(184)

[1] Excluding no replies.

CASELOAD COMPOSITION

Though clearly associated with the use of volunteers, the relative importance of caseload size could not be assessed without reference to caseload composition. We were aware that the client category to which a case may be assigned does not necessarily indicate the amount of work involved. It seemed important, nevertheless, to explore the differences in caseload composition in terms of client categories and their possible relevance to differences in the use of volunteers.

Caseload composition may be analysed in a number of ways. We adopted three. First, we distinguished those caseloads which entirely excluded particular client groups. There were substantial numbers of social workers whose caseloads came into this category. Thus about two in five of the sample did not have any fostering or adoption cases, nor any elderly clients; more than one in three had no clients with mental handicaps or mental illnesses; and one in four or thereabouts were not working with physically handicapped people or with individuals or families with multiple social problems, including that of homelessness (Table 9.3).

Table 9.3   *Composition of caseload; proportion of social workers with client groups not represented in caseload: local authority social workers*

Client group[1]	Proportion of social workers (% of total)
Individuals/families	24
Physically handicapped	25
Children	26
Mentally ill	34
Mentally handicapped	37
Elderly	41
Fostering/adoption	42
Other	40
TOTAL[2]	100
(number)	(817)

[1]   In this and subsequent tables in this chapter and in Appendix VI where client groups are shown, individuals/families relate to those with varied problems including homelessness: the elderly are the unimpaired: and the category 'other' includes children and adults before the courts and the physically ill.
[2]   Excluding no replies.

These trends undoubtedly reflect differences in caseload composition according to caseload size and designation. For example, the majority of social workers in the more senior positions and those with the smallest caseloads are not working with elderly clients while, on the other hand, the majority of social work assistants and those with the larger caseloads do not work with children (see Appendix VI, Tables VI.1 and VI.2).

Secondly, we distinguished caseloads according to their bias as indicated by the extent to which particular client groups represented a substantial part of the total number of clients in the caseload—some 40 per cent or more (Table 9.4).[4] There were considerable variations in the sample in this respect too.

Where caseload bias occurs, however, it is more likely to be towards children and, to a lesser extent, physically handicapped clients, than towards any other client group. It is also more frequent among senior staff and social work assistants and among

Table 9.4 *Composition of caseload; proportion of social workers with client groups representing 40 per cent or more of caseloads: local authority social workers*

Client group	Proportion of social workers (% of total)
Children	20
Physically handicapped	17
Individuals/families	7
Elderly	5
Fostering/adoption	3
Mentally ill	2
Mentally handicapped	2
Others	5
TOTAL[1]	100
(number)	(817)

[1] Excluding no replies.

social workers carrying the smaller and the larger caseloads (Table 9.5 and see Appendix VI, Table VI.3). Thus, among senior staff child-care cases predominate to a greater extent than in the caseloads of any other designation. Among those carrying 100 cases or more, however, and among social work assistants, it is handicapped clients who predominate. These represent on average more than one-half of their total clients. No other caseload size or client group is associated with such a degree of bias. Since some two in five social work assistants, moreover, have such caseloads, no other designation is associated with such a degree of bias.

The evidence of the present inquiry thus suggests that social work assistants, being in the nature of things less likely to extend their activities over a wide range of clients, are the most likely to develop a 'specialised' caseload, particularly in respect of physically handicapped clients. It suggests that, while there may be some ambiguity in the roles of social work assistants and diversity in what they are expected to do, there is tacit agreement in most authorities to use them predominantly for the care of physically handicapped and elderly people. How far this was envisaged in the Younghusband Report (1959) is difficult to know.

Moreover, in so far as children and family problems in some social workers' eyes have a comparatively high status and are among the most preferred client groups, the specialisation of social work assistants would seem to be oriented towards groups who are often regarded as having a lower status and being among the least preferred. Indeed a similar tendency seems to apply to volunteers' activities many of which, as we have seen, show the same bias. Two systems of status hierarchy would seem to operate, in which the low

Table 9.5 *Caseload composition: proportion of social workers where client groups represent 40 per cent or more of caseloads according to designation: local authority social workers*

Client group	Area officers/ deputies, senior social workers	Field workers	Trainees	Social work assistants
		(% of total)		
Children	36	20	7	3
Individuals/families	9	6	16	8
Mentally ill	4	2	0	0
Mentally handicapped	3	2	0	0
Fostering/adoption	14	3	0	0
Elderly	0	3	7	24
Physically handicapped	4	14	7	56
Other	6	5	5	4
TOTAL[1]	100	100	100	100
(number)	(125)	(545)	(57)	(90)

[1] Excluding no replies.

status client groups in the one are matched with their equivalents—social work assistants and volunteers—in the other. That these low status client groups are allocated to the lowest ranks in the social services hierarchy, however, implies a widespread acceptance among social workers that these client groups need less skilled help. Yet there has been no systematic study of the actual social work skills required in this work nor any rational theory advanced as to why it should be easier, more routine or less complex.

It may also be inferred from the analysis that there are considerable variations in caseload composition which are only partly accounted for by the fact that client groups tend to be disproportionately represented in caseloads. There is first, the variable flow of different categories of client, which produces an uneven pattern of referrals. Added to this, there is also the effect of different types of allocation procedure and the extent to which the social workers' choices, preferences, particular interests, experiences or level of expertise determine the allocation of cases. The degree of bias in caseloads presumably arises from a combination of factors, and though 'official' specialisation may be rare at area office level, informal specialisation seems to be more frequent, taking the form of a bias towards one, or sometimes two, client groups, who account for proportionately rather more cases in the total caseload. The important result is that where there is caseload bias in the direction of elderly and physically handicapped clients the proportion of social workers using volunteers tends to be considerably higher than where the caseload bias is towards any other client group.

Caseload Profiles

Thirdly, we distinguished caseloads according to their average composition or the 'profiles'. These profiles were obtained by computing the proportions of the total number of cases represented by each client group in social workers' caseloads. Thus, in the average caseload composition for the sample as a whole children and then physically handicapped clients were the two largest client groups (Table 9.6). Individuals and families with varied problems including homelessness were the third largest. The average caseload thus has more than twice as many children as elderly clients, and almost three times as many physically handicapped people as clients who have mental illnesses or mental handicaps.

Table 9.6   *Average caseload composition: local authority social workers*

Client group	Average % of all cases
Children	22
Physically handicapped	20
Individuals/families	16
Elderly	11
Fostering/adoption	7
Mentally ill	7
Mentally handicapped	7
Other	10
TOTAL[1]	100
(estimated number of cases)	(37,720)

[1] Excluding no replies.

The predominance of children and physically disabled people was evident in the average caseload composition of Southampton's fieldworkers. There is a difference, however, between the results of the two studies. The Southampton social workers had far higher proportions of clients with physical handicaps. This may be due to differences in client classification methods, demographic characteristics and the ways in which the relevant Committees interpret their statutory obligations (Table 9.7).

Very different caseload profiles apply to certain designations. Thus, a sharp contrast is evident between management and senior staff on the one hand and social work assistants on the other. Trainees and fieldworkers occupy an intermediate position and have caseloads that correspond in composition more closely to the average for the sample as a whole (Table 9.8 and see Appendix VI, Table VI.4). By contrast, management and senior staff, as seen earlier, carry much smaller than average proportions of elderly and physically handicapped people, but a much higher proportion of children.

Table 9.7   *A comparison of average caseload composition:
the Southampton study (1976) and the present inquiry
(fieldworkers, social work assistants and trainees):
local authority social workers*

Client group	Southampton[1] NISW (1975)	National sample (BASW 1975)
	(Average % of total cases)	
Children	34	127
Physically handicapped	34	122
Elderly	9	112
Mentally ill	4	17
Mentally handicapped	5	6
All other	14	126
TOTAL	100	100
(estimated number of cases)	5,526	35,670

[1] Neill *et al.*, 'Post-Seebohm social services: (1) The social workers' viewpoint. Perceptions of social workers in four area offices in 1972 and 1975', *Social Work Today*, vol. 8, no. 5 (2 November 1976).

Table 9.8   *Average caseload composition according to designation:
local authority social workers*

Client group	Area officers/ deputies	Senior social workers	Field workers	Trainees	Social work assistants
	(Average % of total cases)				
Children	33	34	23	15	4
Individuals/families	19	16	16	23	11
Fostering/adoption	13	13	8	6	2
Mentally ill	11	7	8	5	3
Physically handicapped	8	9	18	19	43
Mentally handicapped	7	7	7	6	5
Elderly	3	4	9	14	25
Other	6	10	11	12	7
TOTAL[1]	100	100	100	100	100
(estimated number of cases)	(500)	(1,550)	(29,060)	(1,530)	(5,080)

[1] Excluding no replies.

Social work assistants, as already noted, carry the highest average proportion of physically handicapped and elderly clients—their caseloads containing on average more than twice as many physically handicapped and nearly three times as many elderly people as the caseloads of basic-grade social workers. No other client group is as dominant in caseloads as are the physically handicapped in the caseloads of social work assistants. Furthermore, where these clients are combined with elderly people they represent two in three of their current cases.

There are also certain marked differences in the composition of caseloads according to whether or not the social workers concerned (excluding social work assistants) are qualified, mainly because the unqualified fieldworkers are far more likely, on average, to be involved with physically disabled clients. The unqualified also, particularly area officers among them, are, on average, far less likely than their qualified equivalents to have children in their caseloads (Table 9.9).

Table 9.9 *Average caseload composition according to social work qualifications: local authority social workers*

Client group	Qualified	Unqualified	
	Excluding social work assistants and trainees	*Excluding social work assistants and trainees*	*All social work staff*
	(Average % of total cases)		
Children	30	20	18
Individuals/families	17	10	15
Fostering/adoption	10	7	6
Mentally ill	9	7	6
Physically handicapped	8	27	26
Mentally handicapped	7	8	7
Elderly	6	11	13
Other	13	10	9
TOTAL[1]	100	100	100
(estimated number of cases)	(12,230)	(18,880)	(25,490)

[1] Excluding no replies.

There are also differences in average caseload profiles according to size of caseload. Thus, for example, the smaller the caseload the larger the average representation of child-care cases, while the larger the caseload the larger the representation of physically handicapped people (Table 9.10). The same tendencies, though not as strong, apply when caseload size and composition are analysed for fieldworkers only. The smaller and the larger caseloads deviate from the average in their composition and most particularly in the representation of the physically handicapped.

Finally, there are marked differences in the average caseload composition when looked at from the point of view of volunteer use. Users have, on average, higher proportions of physically disabled clients in their caseloads and smaller proportions of

Table 9.10   *Average caseload composition according to caseload size:*
local authority social workers

	Size of caseload				
Client group	*1-19*	*20-39*	*40-59*	*60-99*	*100 or more*
		(Average % of total cases)			
Children	27	24	23	19	6
Individuals/families	21	19	16	13	5
Fostering/adoption	12	7	7	5	3
Physically handicapped	10	14	18	27	55
Elderly	7	9	11	14	15
Mentally ill	6	7	7	7	7
Mentally handicapped	6	7	8	8	3
Other	11	13	10	7	6
TOTAL[1]	100	100	100	100	100
(estimated number of cases)	(1,270)	(6,780)	(10,900)	(12,400)	(6,600)

[1] Excluding no replies.

children. This is not due so much to the influence of social work assistants' caseloads (which do not differ substantially according to use or otherwise of volunteers) but to the higher proportions of physically handicapped clients carried by seniors, fieldworkers and trainees who use volunteers. By contrast, area officers and seniors who are not involved with volunteers, compared with their equivalents who are, are more likely to have much higher proportions of fostering and adoption cases in their caseloads (see Appendix VI, Table VI.5).

THE PROPENSITY TO USE VOLUNTEERS

Since it was evident that there was a link between caseload composition and the use of volunteers, it seemed important that the relative influence of each client group should be assessed. An indication of this relative influence was achieved as follows. First an index (A) was constructed. This was based on dividing the proportions of volunteers whose services were used in the last instance to help particular client groups by the proportion these client groups represented in the average caseloads of those using these volunteers (see Chapter 5, Table 5.4). This showed that elderly clients, though they by no means represent the largest client group, on average, are nevertheless far more likely than other client groups to be helped by volunteers (Table 9.11). Secondly, as a check on this result, an alternative index (B) was similarly constructed, based on the relative frequency with which client groups are helped by volunteers generally (See Chapter 5, Table 5.2). This too showed that elderly clients had a higher propensity than other client groups to be helped by volunteers, but the differences between them and other client groups, particularly clients with physical disabilities, were not nearly so marked as for index A (Table 9.11).

Table 9.11 *Indices of the propensity of client groups to be helped by volunteers: local authority social workers*

Client group	Index A	Index B
Elderly	0·37	0·23
Individuals/families	0·16	0·13
Physically handicapped	0·11	0·19
Mentally ill	0·11	0·17
Children	0·10	0·07
Mentally handicapped	0·08	0·12
Fostering/adoption		0.02
	0·07	
Other		0.07

Thirdly, indices A and B were then each used in turn to weight the average caseload of each designation using volunteers. The indices calculated in this way (C and D) represent for each designation their respective propensities to use volunteers. Each index—C and D—confirmed that social work assistants have the highest propensity to use volunteers (Table 9.12). On the basis of index A, however, they do so mainly because of their elderly clients. On the basis of index B, they use volunteers because they have a higher proportion than anyone else of both elderly and physically handicapped clients.

Table 9.12 *Indices of the propensity of social workers of different designations to use volunteers: local authority social workers*

Designation	Index C	Index D
Social work assistants	17·3	17·5
Trainees	14·7	13·4
Fieldworkers	13·0	12·3
Senior social workers	11·4	10·0
Area officers and deputies	11·2	10·4

At the other extreme, area officers and senior social workers have the lowest propensity to use volunteers because, on average, they have higher proportions of children in their caseloads. The propensity of children to be helped by volunteers on indices A and B is relatively low.

The implications of these findings may be observed in the activities in which volunteers are mostly engaged. Since, for example, the propensity to use volunteers is higher where the representation of particular client groups is higher, then it follows that the deployment of such volunteers, and possibly the scale on which they are used, is influenced accordingly.

REGRESSION ANALYSIS

In order that more accurate quantitative assessments could be made of the association between the use of volunteers and caseload size on the one hand, and caseload composition on the other, a regression analysis of these three variables was undertaken.

Regression equations were calculated with the proportion of social workers using volunteers as the dependent variable and the size of caseloads and the proportions of elderly and of physically handicapped clients, respectively, as the independent variables. The forms of function used and the detailed results are described in Appendix V, Tables V.1, V.2 and V.3.

The results indicate, as shown in Figures 9.2 and 9.3 that the proportions of social workers using volunteers rise more sharply in relation to elderly than to physically handicapped clients, even though the latter represent a greater part of total caseloads, and more sharply in relation to increases in the proportion of each of these client groups than to increases in caseload size.

That the degree of volunteer use is related essentially to the composition of the caseload, rather than to its total size is demonstrated by the results of multiple regression equations, as shown in Appendix V, Table V.3. Thus, an increase for example, of 10 per cent in the proportion of elderly plus physically handicapped clients would be associated on average with an increase of some 2-2½ per cent in the proportion of social workers using volunteers. By contrast, the corresponding increase would be only ½-¾ per cent for a 10 per cent increase in total caseload size.

Two conclusions can be drawn from the regression analysis. First, it would appear that the degree of volunteer use is more sensitive to changes in the proportion of elderly than of physically handicapped clients in the caseload. Secondly, caseload composition is the major determinant of the degree of volunteer use, the size of caseload *per se* being only a relatively minor influence.

TYPES OF SOCIAL WORK INTERVENTION

In order to explore more fully the relevance of the use of volunteers to different aspects of social workers' caseloads, respondents were also asked about the kinds of social work intervention they practised. It seemed reasonable to assume a greater volunteer

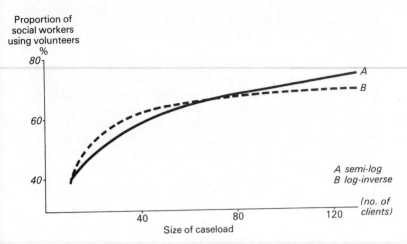

Figure 9.2   *The relationship between the use of volunteers and the size of the caseload: local authority social workers*

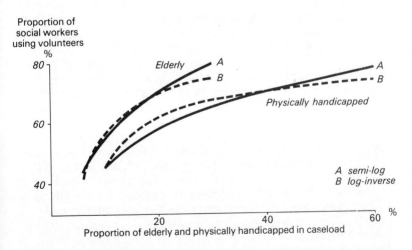

Figure 9.3   *The relationship between the use of volunteers and the proportion of elderly and physically handicapped clients in the caseload*

involvement where the more routine, supportive types of attention were required than where a need was felt for more intensive types of casework. In fact, this assumption was not borne out by our findings.

The difficulty was how to define categories of social work intervention and methods in terms which respondents would find appropriate to their experience. This difficulty was partially resolved by adopting and modifying the four categories of social work intervention which had been tested in the pilot study. These had been developed and were being used experimentally by one of the local authority services departments participating in the inquiry. The four categories were:

(a) active, ongoing intervention by the social worker;
(b) mainly supportive work by the social worker;
(c) support and aid mainly from others, but social worker still in contact or directly supervising;
(d) assessment.

Respondents were asked to indicate how many of their cases in the last full working month came into these four categories. Provision was also made for the respondents to specify, if need be, other types of intervention.

The analysis first showed that the great majority of social workers—indeed almost all—had been involved in active, ongoing intervention, as well as in the mainly supportive types of social work help. Rather fewer—but still the majority—had been involved in the supervision of cases where support and aid were given, mostly by others. Only a minority had been involved in assessment work, and even fewer in other types of intervention. This order of frequency reflects the far higher proportions of clients who were, on average, receiving active and ongoing or mainly supportive types of social work attention as compared with those receiving support and aid mainly from others, or other categories of social work help (Table 9.13).

There were some variations in these general patterns according to designation and caseload size, indicating that caseload bias in client groups, as seen earlier, exists side by side with a degree of bias in the type of social work attention given. Thus, there is likely to be some bias towards active, ongoing intervention for the clients of senior grades and of social workers with smaller caseloads on the one hand, and towards mainly supportive help for the clients of social work assistants and of social workers with larger caseloads on the other (See Appendix VI, Table VI.6). This contrast presumably reflects differences in the composition of their respective caseloads as well as in their qualifications and experience, if not their skills.

Table 9.13   *Average proportions of cases according to types of social work attention given: local authority social workers*

Type of social work attention	Average % of cases
Active, ongoing intervention	38
Mainly supportive work by social worker	38
Aid and support mainly by others	12
Assessment	10
Other	2
TOTAL[1]	100
(estimated number of cases)	(37,550)

[1] Excluding no replies.

No substantial differences emerged, however, in the use of volunteers according to the bias or otherwise in the type of social work attention given.

TIME SPENT ON DIFFERENT TYPES OF
SOCIAL WORK INTERVENTION

It seemed important to try to add something to the picture of caseload activity by obtaining information on the time spent on each type of attention given, not least because of its possible relevance to the use of volunteers.

Necessarily, assessments of time were very approximate, being based on the respondents' own estimates of how much of their time in the last full working week they had spent on each of the four categories of social work intervention. A more meaningful indicator of work demand would probably have been the time spent on each of their cases as such—but the postal method of investigation unfortunately ruled out the collection of such data. The categories used differed slightly from those used for the kind of attention given to cases. They comprised:

(a) assessment work, including diagnosis;
(b) crisis work;
(c) active, ongoing casework;
(d) mobilisation of resources, supportive services and practical assistance.

The analysis shows clearly that active, ongoing casework was far more time consuming than other types of intervention. Relatively few social workers estimated that they had spent as much as one-half of their time on the assessment of cases, crisis work, or the mobilisation of resources.

There were some interesting, though expected, differences in the time spent on each type of caseload activity according to designation and caseload size. Thus, proportionately more social work assistants estimated that they had spent a half or more of their time on the mobilisation of resources, and the same tendency was evident among those with the larger caseloads. The smaller the caseload, however, the less the time spent on crisis work. Moreover, the more senior the post, the lower the proportion of time spent on any of the four categories of caseload activity listed, presumably because of the proportionately greater time spent on management and supervisory duties.

Caseload size, itself in part reflecting social workers' designations, seems to be associated in several ways with the time spent on different activities. First, the smaller the caseload the more likely, in general, that social workers had spent little or no time in crisis work; secondly, social workers with the smallest caseloads were the least likely to have spent as much as a half or more of their time on active, ongoing casework; thirdly, those with the larger caseloads were the most likely to have spent a half or more of their time on the mobilisation of resources.

The main association between the use of volunteers and the amount of time spent in different types of caseload activity seems to arise in respect of the time given to the mobilisation of resources. Here, the proportions of social workers using volunteers is markedly higher among those who have spent as much as one-half of their time on this type of activity than among those who have spent little or none. This tendency may well reflect, however, the greater use of volunteers by social work assistants, more of whom, as we have seen, tended to spend a higher proportion of their time on the mobilisation of resources, since no such differences were apparent among fieldworkers alone.

SOCIAL WORKERS' PREFERENCES

The BASW 1977 Working Party evidently considered that social workers' preferences regarding clients and methods of work were one of the main reasons for welcoming the development of specialisation in social work. It also suggested that 'the denial of these could have deleterious effects on morale'.

It seemed important, in the present inquiry, to trace the extent of any differences between social workers' preferences for client groups and for types of social work activity and what their caseload activities actually were. By these means we hoped it would be possible to explore the relevance of any correspondence between their preferred and actual caseload activities for the use of volunteers.[5]

Preferred Client Groups

Using a precoded list identical to that used in connection with the composition of caseloads, respondents were asked to indicate which particular client groups they would prefer, or prefer not, to work with if they had the choice, or for which groups they had no preference either way.

The analysis showed several interesting features. First, less than one-third of the sample of local authority staff wanted maximum variety in their caseloads, while almost as many had no preference either way. Nearly one in four, however, were evidently against having too varied a caseload and presumably were in favour of a degree of specialisation.

These proportions varied somewhat according to designation, falling proportionately with seniority but hardly at all according to caseload size. Fieldworkers, moreover, were much more likely than any other group to be against too varied a caseload. The figures suggest that attitudes towards mixed caseloads, or towards the degree of mix, vary according to backgrounds, length of experience, status and training. Trainees seem to be more attracted than others to a variety of clients and patterns in their work. This may be one outcome of their more recent professional training.

Secondly, a distinct order of preferences emerged, client groups being ranked, as it were, in order of popularity, (Fig 9.4 and Appendix VI, Table VI.7). The most popular groups are evidently children, fostering and adoption and cases where whole families are involved. Far lower down the scale were elderly and physically handicapped clients. Lowest of all in the rank order of preferences were blind and deaf people, singled out by only very small minorities.

A very similar order of preferences was reported in the Southampton studies (1973 and 1976), the social workers questioned in these studies being far more eager to work with children's problems and interpersonal relationships in the family than to work with elderly and physically disabled people.

Thirdly, it was evident that where client groups were not particularly preferred, it was more usual to find a lack of preference than a preference against. This suggests that substantial proportions of social workers have no strong feelings either way about working with any client group. Nevertheless, there was still an order of relative indifference in the sense that social workers who had no strong preference either way were more likely, for example, to feel this way about people with physical disabilities, including deafness and blindness, than about child-care cases.

Fourthly, though most client groups failed to appeal to only small minorities of social workers, almost one-half of the sample preferred not to work with deaf clients, almost two in five with

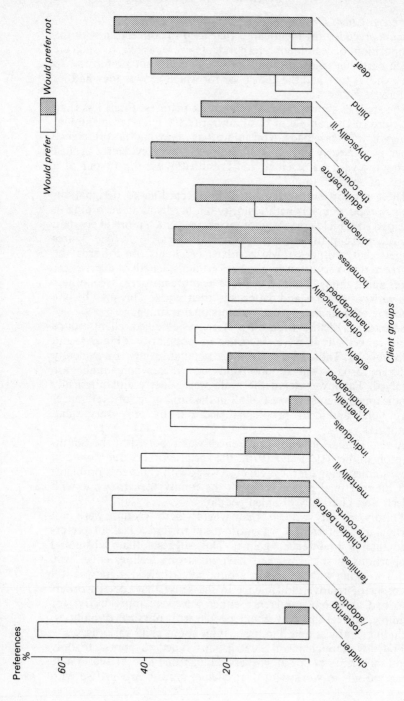

Figure 9.4   Preferences for client groups: local authority social workers

blind people, or adults before the courts, and one-third with homeless people. This suggests that client groups may also be ranked in order of unpopularity.

Generally, with the exception of social work assistants, the preferences for client groups followed the same ranking order, irrespective of designation (and among fieldworkers, irrespective of social work qualifications). Work with children, fostering or adoption cases and families, however, tended to be ranked rather higher by area management staff (perhaps reflecting in some instances their previous child-care training) and senior social workers than by fieldworkers. On the other hand, people who were ill, blind or deaf were ranked rather lower, particularly by area officers, none of whom, evidently, had preferences for working with these client groups.

The order of social work assistants' preferences followed quite a different pattern. First, they have a narrower range, the difference between the most and the least preferred groups being much smaller and less marked. Secondly, they have a different order of priority. Substantially higher proportions of them for example, expressed preferences for work with clients who had physical disabilities (including blindness), with elderly clients and with people who were ill. These particular client groups have generally a much lower appeal for fieldworkers. A similar tendency—namely for the order of preference to be the same, though the range of differences fluctuated—was evident when the preferences were looked at in relation to caseload size. Those with the largest caseloads tended to have the smallest range of preferences and to contain the highest proportions with preferences for work with elderly and physically disabled clients.

Differences in social workers' preferences were not apparently associated in any marked degree with their use of volunteers. This was evident even when, to offset the influence of designation, a separate analysis was made for fieldworkers. The main exceptions were firstly, fieldworkers who wanted to work with blind and deaf clients, who were more likely than others to be using the services of volunteers, in both direct and indirect ways. Secondly, those using the services of volunteers in some way were far less likely than those who were not (even if they had formerly done so) to express a preference for working with children before the courts, or for individuals with varied problems. Generally, however, it was actual rather than preferred caseloads of social workers which seemed to have more influence on their predispositions to use volunteers.

Satisfied Preferences

The degree of correspondence between social workers' preferences for particular client groups, and the presence of these groups in their caseloads, is extremely high. Perhaps social workers come to like what they do. Thus, almost all social workers who prefer to work with physically disabled clients are, in fact, doing so, though by no means exclusively so. The majority of social workers with other preferences are, in addition to any other client groups in their caseloads, also working with their preferred client group. Only among those who most want to work with clients who are physically ill is the proportion actually doing so considerably lower than for those with other preferences (see Appendix VI, Table VI.8).

Thus, it might seem at first glance that there is considerable divergence between preferred and actual caseloads, since the order of client groups in the social workers' caseloads does not always correspond with their order of preferences. This is not so. On the basis of a comparison between the preferred client groups of individual social workers and those with whom they were actually working,[6] the average percentage of satisfied preferences is relatively high—almost 80 per cent.[7] It varies, however, according to designation, being highest for fieldworkers and lowest for social work assistants.

The analysis does not take into account, however, social workers who have client groups in their caseloads with whom they would prefer not to work, or social workers who have fewer of their preferred clients or more of their unpreferred than they would wish. The degree of correspondence shown between preferred and actual client groups is, therefore, only a crude indicator of satisfied preferences.

The degree of satisfied preferences varies according to designation, the average percentage being highest for fieldworkers (81.2) and lowest for social work assistants (68.4). That of senior social workers is no more than 70.6. These differences seem to be due in part to the fact that seniors who would like to work with elderly and physically handicapped people, and social work assistants who would like to work with child care or fostering and adoption cases, are less likely to do so than are fieldworkers with similar preferences.

Social workers who use volunteers appear to be working with their preferred client group or groups more often than non-users. This results in a general tendency for the average percentage of satisfied preferences to be consistently higher where volunteers are used than where they are not. This is particularly so for social work assistants. Similarly, for the sample as a whole, fewer of those who are not working with their preferred groups are using volunteers. This tendency may reflect, in part, the larger average caseloads of social workers who use volunteers. The larger the caseload, the higher the chances that preferred client groups (particularly, as we have seen, those who are elderly or have physical handicaps) will be represented in social workers' caseloads.

Preferred Types of Social Work Intervention

In addition to any preference for particular client groups, social workers were also asked (using the precoded categories identical with those of the time question) to indicate how they felt about the type of social work intervention they most, or least, liked.

Ongoing casework was the most popular, except with social work assistants. Assessment work was a close second, particularly among qualified workers. Lower down the scale of popularity were the mobilisation of resources and crisis work, each accounting for only about one in three social workers' preferences. One in seven and one in five, respectively, preferred not to be involved in either of these activities. The relative appeal of different types of social work intervention was not associated, however, with any differences in the use of volunteers.

THE DOMINANT FACTOR

It has not been possible to examine all the ramifications of social workers' caseloads or the nature of the work generated by different groups of clients, types of problems and types of social work intervention. Nevertheless, the findings strongly suggest that one of the most important factors underlying the use or otherwise of volunteers is the composition of social workers' caseloads and the extent to which these caseloads contain first, elderly, and then physically handicapped, clients.

Thus caseload patterns, and the uneven distribution of those client groups with the higher propensities to be helped by volunteers directly influence which groups of social workers are the most likely to be using volunteers. In other words, the use of volunteers arises partly out of the particular division of labour which has evolved in the local authority social services. The result is clear. Elderly people, who, it must be emphasised, in this study are those without specific handicap, have the highest priority as far as the allocation of volunteers is concerned—higher, indeed, than clients of equivalent ages who are physically handicapped. Yet, on average, elderly people by no means constitute as large a proportion of referrals, allocations or caseloads as clients with physical handicaps.

Caseload patterns have thus emerged as a dominant factor influencing the use of volunteers. This undoubtedly reflects certain implicit beliefs in the profession, if not elsewhere, concerning the needs of elderly (and to a lesser extent physically handicapped) clients, for which the contribution of the volunteer is felt to be the best and most appropriate fit.

These beliefs, and the division of labour which is linked with them, are likely to be further reinforced if the recommendations of the Birch Committee (1976) on the use of qualified workers, and the suggestions of the BASW Working Party (1977) on the definition of social work, come to be widely adopted. The Working Party see the development of social work not only as 'clearly tied to the growth of specialisation'. They also see this specialisation as closely linked with the 'personal skills' informed by 'professional values' and used in the context of 'interpersonal relationships', all of which, in their view, distinguishes the function of social work from that of social services and the qualified from the unqualified social worker. The effect of such distinctions, however, may be to fragment rather than to integrate all those activities which have come to be commonly understood as social work today, and to differentiate yet more sharply than our evidence suggests, groups of social workers according to the clients they work with and their use of volunteers.

SUMMARY

Size and Composition of Caseloads

The evidence of the present inquiry shows that there is considerable variation both in the size and in the composition of caseloads among local authority social workers, particularly in relation to designation. Thus, while for the sample as a whole the average number of cases carried was forty-six, the average caseload size was more than twice as high for fieldworkers and social work assistants as for those in management or senior posts.

The smaller the caseload, however, the larger, on average, the proportionate representation of child-care cases. By contrast, the largest caseloads tended to contain much higher proportions, on average, of clients who were physically handicapped in some way.

Average caseload composition for the sample as a whole, however, shows that children and physically handicapped people are the two largest client groups, each representing about one in five of all cases. The result is that there are on average twice as many child-care cases as elderly clients, and almost as many physically handicapped people as clients with mental illnesses and mental handicaps.

Substantial proportions of social workers, however, have caseloads which entirely exclude certain client groups. Relatively small proportions of senior or area officers work with elderly people, just as relatively few social work assistants work with children or fostering and adoption cases. Some degree of caseload bias is evident among a minority of the sample, and this occurs most often among social work assistants in respect of physically handicapped clients. Qualified and unqualified staff also differ in the composition of their caseloads.

Use of Volunteers

There is a very marked association between the size of caseloads and their composition and the use of volunteers. Thus the incidence of volunteer use rises as caseload size increases and the proportion of elderly and handicapped clients increases. An assessment of the relative influence of each client group on volunteer use suggests that elderly clients have the greatest propensity to be helped by volunteers. The results of a regression analysis confirmed this. First, the influence of caseload composition is significantly greater than that of caseload size. Secondly, the degree of volunteer use appears to be more sensitive to change in the proportion of elderly than of physically handicapped clients.

Preferences

A distinct order of preference is evident among social workers in respect of the client groups with whom they would most like to work. The most popular groups are children, fostering and adoption cases and cases where families are involved. Less popular are physically handicapped clients, particularly the blind and the deaf. Only social work assistants have a different order of preferences, being more likely than others to want to work with people who have physical handicaps.

The degree of correspondence between social workers' preferences and their actual caseloads is relatively high, while the percentage of satisfied preferences tends to be higher among users of volunteers than among non-users. This is partly because of the generally larger caseloads of the users.

NOTES

1 The list of client groups was identical with that used earlier in the questionnaire (see Chapter 5).

2 Apart from published studies such as those by Neill *et al.* (1973, 1976) the present researchers were able to consult the results of several unpublished studies carried out for their own internal use by social services departments' research units.

3 An analysis of the extent to which the number of volunteers involved and clients helped increased with caseload size could be only made for 'direct' users. This showed no consistent trend, the scale of voluntary help fluctuating. Nevertheless, on average, more volunteers were used and more cases helped where caseloads were over 60, than where they were under 20.

4 The sixteen client groups used in the questionnaire were reduced to eight by combining appropriate client groups (such as, for example, all physically handicapped groups) and expressing the number of cases in each of the eight groups as percentages of the total number of cases in each social worker's caseload. In the analysis, the percentages were grouped in deciles.

5 An indication of satisfied preferences regarding client groups was obtained by comparing the preferences of social workers with the composition of their actual caseloads, and then calculating the 'average' degree of satisfied preferences.

6 The curve indicating social workers' preferences (A) does indeed diverge from the curve indicating the proportion of social workers whose caseloads include the client groups indicated (B); but the comparison is misleading, since the data upon which the two variables, A and B, are based is not one for one. The proportion of social workers with, for example, elderly people in their caseloads does not necessarily correspond with the proportion of social workers who would prefer to work with this group. The curve (C), however, is based on isomorphic data, and indicates the proportions in each group of social workers with specific preferences who have, in addition to other clients, their preferred client group in their caseloads, and is a much nearer indication of the degree of satisfied preferences.

7 This was based on using weighted averages, according to the proportions of social workers with preferences for each client group who had such client groups in their caseloads and the numbers of social workers expressing preferences for each client group.

10 The Division of Labour

INTRODUCTION

INTRODUCTION

The administration of social work has taken on special significance from the reorganisation of the social services in 1971. Much larger departments were set up, a new structure of social work personnel was introduced and, at the same time, in response to changes in social legislation, new forms of social work practice and methods of managing the work flow were established.

The scope of the present inquiry has obliged us to limit our view of these factors and their possible association with the use of volunteers, and to place our main emphasis on the organisation of the work flow in those area offices covered by the supplementary data.[1]

REFERRALS AND ALLOCATIONS

Scale

We first examined the scale of client referrals to area offices, and their allocation to social work staff during the previous month. These we regarded as important though crude indicators of the volume of work in area offices, even though the data related only to the previous month, and did not allow for fluctuations over time.

Interestingly enough, however, the incidence of volunteer use was hardly affected as the number of referrals increased, except where these exceeded 300. In these instances, the proportion of social workers using volunteers rose noticeably from just over one-half to two-thirds. A similar, though sharper rise was evident as the scale of monthly allocations increased, but there it occurred when the number of allocations exceeded 200 (Table 10.1).

There were, however, relatively few area offices where referrals or allocations reached these numbers. In the majority of offices, monthly referrals were fewer than 200 and allocations no more than 100, the averages for the sample as a whole being just over 150 referrals and just under 100 allocations per month respectively.

The scale of referrals was directly related to the number of social work staff in the area office, the average number of referrals rising as the number of social work staff increased—from just over 120 referrals in offices of under fifteen staff to just over 200 in offices of over thirty staff. The same tendency, but to a less marked degree, could be observed in the average number of monthly allocations.

Table 10.1   *Scale of monthly referrals and allocations and the use of volunteers: local authority area offices*

Scale	Monthly referrals (% of total)	% of social workers using volunteers	Monthly allocations (% of total)	% of social workers using volunteers
Fewer than 100	26	48	65	51
101-200	52	46	27	42
201-300	16	53	7	66
Over 300	6	66	–	–
TOTAL	100	100	100	100
(number of social workers)	(· ·)	(608)	(· ·)	(530)
(estimated number of cases)	(15,700)	(· ·)	(11,300)	(· ·)
Mean	153		98.4	

Area offices also varied considerably in the extent to which allocations represented all or only part of the total monthly referrals. In only one in six offices were all the referrals in the previous month allocated to social work staff while, at the other extreme, in one in five offices fewer than one-half of the month's referrals had been allocated. For the sample as a whole, the total of allocated cases represented some 72 per cent of all referrals, though there were variations in this, too, according to the size of the unit—the highest average proportion being in the smallest unit with the smallest number of referrals. There is, however, no apparent association between the proportion of referrals allocated to social workers in the different area offices and the incidence of volunteer use among them.

Further analysis was made of the scale of referrals and allocations in relation first, to the number of social workers actually available and secondly, to the full complement, assuming all outstanding vacancies were filled. This showed that, if anything, the proportions of social workers using volunteers declined as the average number of referrals and of new allocations per social worker actually available rose.

This suggests that, while greater numbers of referrals and allocations in area offices, as we have seen, may be associated with higher proportions of social workers using volunteers, this is not so when these numbers impose a greater workload on existing staff than would have been the case if all outstanding vacancies were filled. Thus, as Table 10.2 shows, though on the basis of a full staff complement, the average number of allocations per social worker would have been smaller (8.1) than the corresponding referrals

(10.4), on the basis of the actual staff in post, average allocations were greater (11.5). This is the equivalent of an increase of 42 per cent in the workload, as measured by the average number of new allocations per existing staff. These disparities give some indication of the additional work carried by workers in offices where there are outstanding vacancies.[2]

Table 10.2   *Average monthly referrals and allocations per social workers and use of volunteers: local authority area offices*

Average number per social worker per month	Referrals: Full staff quota	Allocations		% of social workers using volunteers
		Full staff quota	Actual staff	
		(% of total)		
Fewer than 5	11	31	8	51
5-10	51	46	48	
11-15	27	16	23	47
16-20	7	5	14	
21-25	1	1	5	
26-30	1	1	—	42
over 30	2	—	2	
TOTAL[1]	100	100	100	100
(number of offices)	(90)	(81)	(83)	(··)
(number of social workers)	(··)	(··)	(··)	(530)
Mean	10·4	8·1	11·5	(··)

[1] Excluding no replies.

Composition

We then examined the composition of referrals and allocations by computing averages for the whole sample. This showed that the three client groups most frequently referred to area offices were first, individuals and families with varied problems, including homelessness; secondly, people with physical disabilities; and thirdly, elderly people. Next, were children, followed in relatively small proportions by people with mental illnesses, mental handicaps and with other problems and difficulties (Table 10.3).

The pattern hardly changes for allocations, except that there are relatively more physically handicapped clients and proportionately fewer individuals and families with varied problems allocated to social work staff than had originally been referred to area offices. This is perhaps because, for the latter client group, agencies other than the statutory social services may have been called upon for help.

In comparing the average composition of social workers' case-loads with the average composition of one month's allocations, the

Table 10.3   *Composition of average monthly referrals, allocations and caseloads: local authority area offices*

Client group	Average referrals	Average allocations (% of total cases)	Average caseloads
Individuals/families	20	17	15
Physically handicapped	19	22	21
Elderly (unimpaired)	18	19	12
Children	12	12	21
Fostering/adoption	5	5	7
Mentally ill	6	6	7
Mentally handicapped	4	4	6
Other	16	15	11
TOTAL	100	100	100
(estimated number of cases)	(12,100)	(8,700)	(24,730)

most striking difference is in the relative proportions of children. These represent on average a relatively small part of allocations, but a relatively large part of caseloads. By contrast, elderly clients represent a larger part of referrals than of average caseloads.[3]

THE FLOW OF WORK

In the previous chapter we noted and discussed caseload patterns, the uneven distribution of client groups in caseloads, and the special significance of these distributions for the use of volunteers. We thought it would be of interest, if only on the basis of one month's intake, to trace the progress of client groups from referral to allocation and thus to show how, on average, the accepted referrals are distributed between social workers according to their designation, qualifications and the use of volunteers.

First, it is evident that while the majority of all client groups referred to area offices are accepted and accordingly allocated to the staff, the proportions allocated vary. This, presumably, is a partial consequence of the varying statutory obligations of social services departments towards different client groups. Thus, on average, higher proportions of clients with physical handicaps are accepted than individuals and families with varied problems, including homelessness.

Secondly, there is considerable variation between client groups in the average time each is likely to remain in the social workers' current caseloads, children tending to remain the longest. This would explain why they come to represent, on average, a substantial part of caseloads, in spite of the fact that they constitute a relatively small proportion of total referrals and allocations. Thus, children tend to have the lowest propensity to be helped by volunteers, while elderly clients—who tend to be the shorter-term cases—have the highest. It may be that the use of volunteers enables social workers to shorten the time elderly people remain 'active' in their caseloads. Volunteers may also be more easily available and considered more suitable for short-term than for long-term commitments. The longer-term cases tend to require a degree of continuity that volunteers may not be able to guarantee. Moreover, much of the work with children presumes not only skill and experience, but constant review and assessment. Social workers may feel that the involvement of volunteers in some of this work is too complicated and risky.

Thirdly, it is evident that there is an uneven distribution of cases between social work staff, not only in general, but also for each client group. The result is that the chances of clients being allocated to a senior social worker for example, or to a qualified worker, as well as being helped by volunteers, varies for each client group. This is shown in the analysis (based on estimates of their respective share of each client group) of the flow of cases between different designations, between qualified and unqualified social workers, and between the users and non-users of volunteers. Fieldworkers naturally take by far the major share of all clients—almost three-quarters—though they represent only two-thirds of the social worker sample. There are, however, some variations in this general pattern according to each client group (Table 10.4). Thus for example, management and senior staff tend to have a larger share of children, cases of fostering and adoption, and mentally ill clients than they do of others. On the other hand, social work assistants, as we have already seen, have a greater share than others of elderly and physically handicapped clients.

The analysis also shows that when allocated to fieldworkers these two client groups are much more likely to go to the unqualified than to the qualified workers.[4] The result is that if the shares of the unqualified fieldworkers and social work assistants are combined, then over four-fifths of elderly clients, and more than three-quarters of all physically handicapped clients, go to those staff who are unqualified in the social work sense. While this is partly due to the relatively high proportion of unqualified fieldworkers in the sample (reflecting national proportions), a somewhat different situation applies to children, where the combined share of the unqualified workers is smaller—just over one-half.

Social workers who use volunteers have generally a somewhat higher share of total cases than the non-users. The differences are particularly marked in the client groups with the highest propensity to be helped by volunteers—the elderly and the physically handicapped. As illustrated in Figure 10.1, the number of these clients

Table 10.4 *Proportion of clients allocated according to client group and designation: local authority social workers*

Client group	Area officers, deputies and seniors	Field workers	Trainees	Social work assistants	Total (estimated number of cases)
	(% of total in each client group)				
Fostering/ adoption	12	80	4	4	100 (1,830)
Children	11	83	3	3	100 (5,090)
Mentally ill	10	81	3	6	100 (1,820)
Mentally handicapped	7	78	4	11	100 (1,650)
Individuals/ families	7	76	7	10	100 (3,850)
Physically handicapped	3	64	4	29	100 (5,180)
Elderly (unimpaired)	2	60	6	32	100 (2,750)
Other	5	79	6	10	100 (2,560)
TOTAL	7	75	5	13	100 (24,730)

allocated to users of volunteers is more than twice those allocated to non-users. What is not clear, however, is whether this results from an allocation of clients to social workers who already use volunteers, or from the greater propensity to use volunteers by social workers to whom these clients are allocated.

Client groups thus seem to have distinctive 'careers' as far as their access to social work staff is concerned. They do not have the same chance of being accepted by social services departments or, if they are accepted, of being allocated to social workers who are equivalent in their status, their qualifications, or in their propensity ·to use volunteers. This is illustrated in the 'career' patterns of three client groups shown in Figure 10.2.

These 'careers', however, are not just simply the results of operational procedures, since the procedures themselves—including the allocation of cases, the use of different grades of social work staff, and the degree of specialisation—seem to vary according to the differences in the way clients' needs are assessed and according to the person making the assessment (Smith and Harris, 1972). The Smith and Harris study showed for example, that the more self-evident the need and the greater the emphasis on the relief function of the agency, the more routine the allocation procedures and the duties of the social work staff. Our findings also suggest that such considerations play some part in determining the outcome of

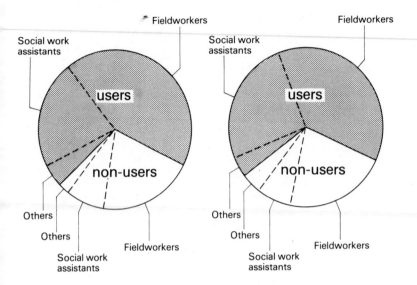

Figure 10.1 *The allocation of physically handicapped and elderly clients to users and non-users of volunteers*

clients' careers, depending where they come in a 'hierarchy' of assumed needs. These needs, which have by no means been examined or tested for their validity, have apparently become one of the most important guidelines for the division of labour in social services departments. As the BASW Working Party (1977) suggests, with supporting evidence, social service agencies traditionally 'tend to define need in terms of categories of clients'. In advocating a more flexible approach, the Working Party has proposed three criteria for work allocation which would help determine the levels of skill and service—in particular of the qualified worker—required in any given circumstances. These are the level of client vulnerability, the degree of case complexity and the significance of decision making. These might, if universally adopted, introduce new definitions of client need. If, however, as seems likely, these new definitions come to be associated with different levels and categories of social work which have, in social workers' eyes, different status values, the result would be the creation of a new hierarchy with little more validity than before.

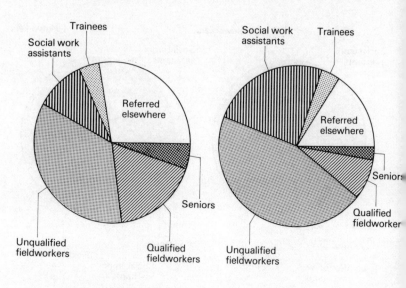

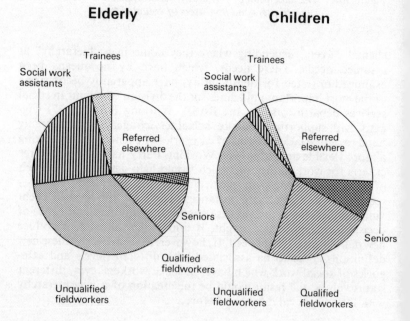

Figure 10.1   *Flow patterns of clients referred to local authority offices*

SUMMARY

On the basis of the figures for one month, area offices, at the time of the inquiry, appear to have had an average of just over 150 referrals, of which just under three-quarters were allocated to social work staff. There is a tendency for the incidence of volunteer use to be highest where the number of monthly referrals and allocations exceeds 300 and 200, respectively. It appears that the effect of outstanding vacancies in local authority area offices is to increase the workload, as measured by the average number of new allocations per existing staff, by some 40 per cent.

The composition of monthly referrals and allocations shows that the most frequently represented are individuals and families with varied problems including homelessness, people with physical disabilities, and elderly people. Physically handicapped clients are the most and individuals and families the least likely to be allocated to social workers, each client group having a different propensity to be accepted by the area office in question. There is also considerable variation in the average time each client group remains in social workers' caseloads, the longest-term case being children and the shortest-term, elderly clients.

An analysis of the distribution of cases among social workers showed that client groups have distinctive 'careers' as far as their access to social work staff is concerned, each having a different chance of being allocated to social workers who are equivalent in their status, qualifications, or propensity to use volunteers. Elderly and physically handicapped clients are more likely for example, to be allocated to unqualified than to qualified social workers and to social workers who use volunteers.

NOTES

1 Other aspects of work organisation in relation to the use of volunteers were considered and are contained in the full Report. These were: allocation procedures, and the number, function and composition of social work teams within the area offices.
2 Area offices varied considerably in the number of their outstanding vacancies some experiencing greater difficulties than others in filling posts or in the rate of staff turnover. In only just over one-quarter of the offices were there no vacancies at all at the time of the inquiry. In two-fifths, outstanding vacancies accounted for up to 20 per cent of the total staff, and in one in ten offices, for 30 per cent or more. The average proportion of unfilled vacancies (in relation to the total staff for the sample as a whole) was just under 10 per cent. However, the proportion of social workers using volunteers evidently falls once there are any outstanding vacancies at all. Thereafter, the proportions of such vacancies do not seem to influence matters to any important degree. It is difficult to know how far this is because all vacancies, no matter what their number, add to the workload of existing staff in some way.

3 It was thought of interest to estimate the average monthly referrals and allocations of area offices in Great Britain as well as the estimated numbers of cases carried by the total social worker population. These estimates are, of course, very approximate, since they are based on the assumption that the average size and composition of caseloads (and of average referrals and allocations) in the general social worker population corresponds closely with that in the sample. If this were so, then it would appear that in mid-summer 1975—the time to which the data relate—local authority social workers were probably carrying in total one million or so cases, more than one-half of which were children, physically handicapped and elderly people—for each of whom the local authorities concerned may have had a statutory responsibility. Moreover, on the basis of an average annual turnover in clients of at least 4.3 (assuming the average stay of 2.8 months per client in the caseloads of the sample population applies generally) then the total number of clients carried by the social worker population employed in the local authority services in Britain for a twelve-month period may be well over 4 million, of whom over 2 million are people who are physically handicapped or elderly or children. It has been estimated that at least one in three cases are clients who have had previous contact with social services departments and are not, therefore, 'new' clients to the services. An approximate estimate of one month's flow of 'new' clients is probably between 500,000 and 666,000 and that of one year between 2 and 3 million. This represents about 5 per cent of the total population of Great Britain in mid-1975 (Registrar General, 1975). It is perhaps in the light of this volume of work, crudely measured in terms of numbers of clients only (and leaving out of account the grossing factors involved) that the present and anticipated cuts in manpower and other resources in the social services may be assessed, as well as the contribution of the voluntary worker. As we have seen, the estimated number of cases being helped by volunteers may be about 70,000 at any one time. On the basis of the scale of work indicated here, this represents no more than 7 per cent of the total monthly caseloads of local authority social work staff.

4 Fewer than one in three offices were working with a complement of mostly qualified staff, while in the same proportion of offices, qualified staff were in the minority. This, evidently, was partly because there were vacancies still outstanding. On the assumption that these were filled by qualified staff, then the proportion of offices with mostly qualified staff would rise sharply to over two-fifths, and those working with mostly unqualified staff would fall to under one-quarter —an overall rise of 36 per cent in the proportions of qualified staff of the total. The ratio of qualified to unqualified staff was not associated with the use of volunteers.

11 Pressures and Priorities

INTRODUCTION

No one, as far as we know, has yet succeeded in assessing the caseload of the social worker by the demands it makes, in terms not only of individual time and energy but also of personal stress and worry. Many attempts are being made to develop an objective system of measurement, and the importance of doing so is underlined by our evidence, which suggests that the distribution of caseloads by size and composition, and therefore of social work activity, is very uneven.

Though we could not in the present inquiry attempt to measure work demands, we did feel it important to find out how social workers themselves assessed them and what were their suggestions for improving the service. We thought also that their views in both these respects might be relevant to the use of volunteers.

PRESSURES OF WORK[1]

It is widely acknowledged that the staff of social services departments work under varying degrees of pressure, partly as a result of the number and type of referrals that come to area offices in relation to the staff available. This has been confirmed in several studies. In the Southampton studies (Neill *et al* 1973, 1976) for example, the majority of fieldworkers felt they worked under considerable or severe pressure. This pressure is seen as affecting both the way in which staff work and the extent to which they have to postpone or leave undone work which they feel they ought to do.

We thought it important to ask social workers about the pressure of time, particularly since in the pilot study some social workers who did not use voluntary help had said that this was because they did not have the time to supervise the volunteers' activities. Yet it by no means followed that those with plenty of time, or at least enough, were necessarily drawing upon voluntary help. Respondents were asked, therefore, as were social workers in the Southampton inquiries, to indicate in precoded replies, which of four types of time and pressure situation they felt corresponded with their present feelings about their work.

There were comparatively few respondents who found they had plenty of time to do what they felt ought to be done. The majority of local authority social workers, as in other studies, felt that they worked under considerable pressure, nearly one in three to the point where they felt they had not nearly enough time to do their work as they thought it ought to be done (Table 11.1). A more or less equivalent proportion, however, felt that they could get through their work by keeping hard at it all the time. A very similar pattern was evident in the replies of probation officers, indicating that in the two services views on the pressures of work are not too dissimilar. There is also a fairly close correspondence between the replies of fieldworkers in the Southampton study (1976) and in the present inquiry, though somewhat higher proportions in the national sample than in Southampton felt under considerable pressure.

Table 11.1 *Pressure of work and designation: local authority social workers*

Type of pressure	Area officers/ deputies (number)	Senior social workers	Field workers	Trainees	Social work assis- tants	Total
				(% of total)		
Considerable pressure: not nearly enough time to do work as it ought to be done	(12)	44	38	20	18	32
work falling into arrears occasionally	(13)	31	26	13	29	28
Just about get through by keeping hard at it	(4)	20	28	43	43	32
Plenty of time to do comfortably what ought to be done	(2)	3	6	24	10	7
No reply		2	2	–	–	1
TOTAL[1][2] (number)	(..) (31)	100 (108)	100 (583)	100 (61)	100 (105)	100 (888)

[1] Caseload holders only.

Feelings about time pressures evidently vary considerably according to designation. Those in senior and management positions were much more likely than others, for example, to feel they worked under considerable pressure, and almost one-half of senior social workers found that they did not have time to do their job as they felt it ought to be done. Social work assistants and trainees, on the other hand, were much more likely to feel that they could just get through their work if they kept hard at it, and fewer of them, particularly of trainees, felt they worked under considerable pressure. Trainees, in fact, are the only designation which contains a sizeable minority who felt they could get through their work comfortably, presumably a reflection of the relatively lighter loads placed on some of the newer recruits to social work, in contrast to the burdens of seniority. Even so, as many as one in three trainees felt they worked under considerable pressure, as did nearly one-half of social work assistants.

Caseload size, however, was not such an important factor as might have been assumed. True, the great majority of those who got through their work comfortably had caseloads of under forty cases, whereas most of those working under considerable pressure had caseloads in excess of this number. Yet the differences, according to caseload size, particularly between the highest-sized and the intermediate-sized caseloads, were not all that marked. Furthermore, the majority of social workers, irrespective of the number of cases they carried, still felt they worked under considerable pressure.

The Southampton studies (1973 and 1976) suggested that feelings of time pressure experienced by most of the fieldworkers questioned were perhaps only marginally related to current workloads. There was also the question as to whether the work was perceived to be worthwhile and appropriate. The social workers also argued that there was not necessarily a causal link between the size of the caseload and the amount of work that had to be done. Any assessment of the demands that social work makes probably needs to be related, therefore, to the nature and amount of social work activity that is undertaken, as well to the time that is spent.

Such considerations may well underlie the fact that the type of work pressure felt by social workers does not seem to be a factor which encourages or discourages the use of voluntary help. This finding is of some interest. It might have been assumed that social workers who felt the most pressure would have found things easier if they had used voluntary help. It seems that this may not be so, since when voluntary help is utilised, the proportion of social workers experiencing considerable pressure remains relatively unchanged.

It should also be emphasised that the pressures felt by social workers may not all arise from their casework, or be of the kind that could be reduced or ameliorated by allocating volunteers to specific types of cases or activities. Work pressure may be accentuated by the nature of the referrals, particularly by the proportions of statutory referrals, including those of child care. As we have seen, social workers working with children are far more reluctant to use voluntary help, tending to feel that such cases are not appropriate for volunteers, or that they are not within the capacity of most of the voluntary helpers available. Policy and organisational factors—relating to their own as well as to other agencies—also contribute to the pressures on social workers. Where they do, their effect is hardly likely to be diminished through voluntary help.

LEVELS OF STRESS [2]

Just as it seemed likely that work pressures would have some bearing on the use of volunteers, so too with stresses and worries arising from work. A likely assumption, partly arising from our preparatory discussions, seemed to be that volunteers might be less frequently used where social workers felt under stress, since any extra work entailed in using voluntary help would be the last straw. We wished to test this assumption. Respondents were asked, therefore, to assess—in their own terms and by their own standards—their levels of stress and worry over their work during the last working month, and to comment if they wished. It was recognised that the question (itself used in a social services department's experimental study) was an extremely subjective one and that the replies might not necessarily be related to work factors alone. No direct association, however, between stress levels and the use of volunteers emerged.

Over two in five social workers assessed their level of stress and worry over work matters as high, a substantial proportion as at a medium level, and a small minority as low (mostly 'quite' rather than 'very' low) (Table 11.2). Those who experienced the higher

Table 11.2　*Level of stress and designation:*
local authority social workers

Level of stress	Area officers/ deputies (number)	Senior social workers	Field workers	Trainees	Social work assistants	Total
				(% of total)		
Very high	(7)	15	9	5	3	9
Quite high	(11)	41	38	43	28	37
Medium	(11)	39	40	36	55	41
Quite low and very low	(2)	5	11	16	13	11
No reply	(–)	–	2	–	1	2
TOTAL[1]	(··)	100	100	100	100	100
(number)	(31)	(108)	(583)	(61)	(105)	(888)

[1] Caseload holders only.

levels of stress tended to carry, on average, larger caseloads than those who assessed their stress levels as low. But the differences according to caseload size were not very marked, rather confirming the view that it is, perhaps, not so much the number of cases carried which contributes to stress as the proportion of very demanding cases in any given caseload.

IDEAS FOR IMPROVING SERVICES TO CLIENTS

There were three reasons for asking respondents to suggest one idea for improving social work services to clients.[3] First, the question was intended to give them an opportunity to add to the comments they may have made in reply to the earlier questions about their satisfactions and dissatisfactions with their work. Secondly, it seemed important to discover from social workers themselves what they thought were the priorities for improving services. In both these respects the response of social workers suggested that they welcomed the opportunity to put forward their ideas. Thirdly, it was hoped that the replies would indicate the extent to which the contribution of volunteers was seen as a means of improving social work services.

There was, in the event, hardly any reference to volunteers. Only seventeen local authority social workers and three probation officers of the total sample of over 1,400 mentioned them at all. One or two practical schemes were suggested, such as that by one area officer, who proposed a 'local budget of a reasonable amount' to be given to 'each operational social service unit, to use at immediate and local discretion to assist, prime and support any voluntary activity'. But generally it seems as if the work of voluntary helpers is not seen by social workers as central to the improvement of present services.

Much greater priority, as can be seen from Table 11.3, is given to other measures, particularly to changes in social work practice; to more and better resources, including more staff; to improvements in the structure and organisation of social services departments; and to the broader issues of social policy. Far less often mentioned were ideas concerning the community.

Changes in Social Work Practice
Changes in social work practice, including methods of approach, were proposed by over one-third of the local authority social workers and over one-half of probation officers. Thus it is in the practice of their profession that the social workers most often see the need for change, particularly in their roles and methods of work.

Some respondents thought that services could be improved by a

Table 11.3 *Ideas for improving social work services to clients*

Ideas for improving service	Local authority social workers (% of total)	Probation officers
Changes in social work practice		
roles and performance of social workers	18	17
standards of practice and training	10	18
the workload	6	19
sub-total	34	54
More and better resources		
specific	10	13
general	8	9
staff	8	11
sub-total	26	33
Changes in structure and organisation		
hierarchy, bureaucracy, management, etc.	10	13
conduct of service, administration, decentralisation, etc.	8	15
sub-total	18	28
Changes in social policy	8	15
Other (including references to volunteers and to the community)	9	7
None	14	14
No reply	8	1
TOTAL[1]	100	100
(number)	(1,220)	(203)

[1] Multiple replies.

general reappraisal of the social worker's task—a 'change in the philosophy of the whole profession'. Others raised the matter of the social worker's personal qualities and attitudes. Two topics of current interest received some mention. These are the need in the local authority services first, for a career grade, and secondly, for the development of specialisation. Typical of such ideas was the comment of an area officer who wished to 'shatter the myth of the generic social worker by actively encouraging specialisms both within and outside the team structure'. Sometimes, however, it was believed that both approaches were valuable and should be retained. Thus one social worker suggested 'more specialisation within a generic department'; and another, 'the return to specialisation, but retaining generic teams covering set areas'.

Other methods and approaches were suggested as ways of improving services to clients though the emphasis varied. Sometimes it was on 'prevention', (one idea here was the introduction of 'family aides') and sometimes on client or community involvement. Another suggestion was the 'development of private practice in the casework service'.

Probation officers more often found room for improvement in standards of social work practice and training than local authority social workers. They emphasised the need for trained workers, both before and after recruitment and the necessity for education in 'specific styles of working', for 'better communications' and the need for 'a greater degree of liaison, and acceptance that other agencies have a valid point of view'.

Comparatively few local authority social workers—mainly fieldworkers—but nearly one in five probation officers made suggestions concerning their workload. In many instances, smaller or different types of caseload were proposed, but there were also references to the reorganisation of work in terms of reducing the frequency of visits to clients, and to making hours of work more flexible.

More and Better Resources

As seen earlier, many social workers are concerned about the lack of resources in the statutory services. In suggesting improvements in these services, more than one in four local authority social workers and one in three probation officers referred to the need for more resources or to improvements in the way present resources are used.

Sometimes the suggestions made were of a fairly generalised character which, as well as proposing 'more and better', also proposed improvements in the distribution of resources and the matching of resources to need. There were also references to improving staff shortages, personnel being seen as a vital resource.

More often specific ideas were put forward, such as the use in holiday periods of school premises as 'community centres to cater for adolescents', or the provision of more support for young mothers and small children through 'classes in parentcraft, mothers' clubs, marital counselling, etc'.

Structure and Organisation

Nearly one in five of local authority social workers and over one in four probation officers felt that improvements in social work services to clients could be brought about by changes in the structure and organisation of their departments or offices in two directions.

First, there were references to changes required in what were often described as hierarchical and bureaucratic structures. Suggestions were made for 'flattening out' these structures, for taking social work 'out of the local authority bureaucracy', to reducing 'middle management' and developing the 'sharing of decision making'. Many social workers favoured a more flexible open and adaptable system, as indeed they had argued before the reorganisation of the services, rather than the hierarchical one which they feel has since developed.

There were also other suggestions—such as 'the establishment of a two-tier system, where many of the 'form-filling procedures' and 'means-tested applications' could be dealt with by social work assistants or administrators; or of a 'mobile advice-only service covering the widest range of advice, including citizens advice bureau resources'. A few respondents went further, suggesting more radical changes such as taking the social services 'out of the hands of local authorities', 'standardising the services' as much as possible by 'setting up a national board', and establishing a 'quite distinct profession'. Social workers would be individually responsible for their work and not answerable to 'a hierarchy' but to their 'own professional body—BASW'.

The second direction of change was that explicitly related to organisational features. Decentralisation was a recurrent theme, as was the need for smaller departments and greater autonomy at 'area office level'. One social worker suggested that there should be one team who were 'completely free of statutory cases'—and several others thought that the setting up of 'intake teams' would improve things.

Other Ideas

Another group of ideas—particularly among area management staff—focused on changes relating to policy decisions involving other agencies or central government, often requiring new legislation for their implementation. There were far-ranging suggestions, such as 'diverting the defence budget', 'paying mothers to stay at home to look after their children', or 'abolishing the juvenile court'. Other suggestions were for voluntary organisations to be incorporated more 'within the local authority set-up', for the encouragement of community involvement; and for an adequate salary structure to establish more stability in area teams. There were also references to the need for closer and more effective links between the DHSS and local authority social services departments.

Only a small proportion in both samples had no particular ideas. This was especially true of those over 54, though the social worker who was 'too pessimistic' even to consider that it was worth mentioning any ideas was in fact aged somewhere between 25 and 34.

The Use of Volunteers

Not only were volunteers hardly referred to in social workers' ideas for improving services but there seems little distinction between users and non-users in their ideas. Far greater emphasis is given to other improvements, particularly to professional matters relating to the practice of social work. Perhaps in the last analysis social workers are simply being realistic. Without underestimating the possible contribution of volunteers, they cannot make up for scarcities in vital resources or shortcomings in the structure and organisation of social services today. Indeed, there may be less potential for the development of closer collaboration between volunteer and professional particularly in view of the deficiencies in social service provision as these are perceived by local authority social workers, and in the basic conditions under which they feel social work is practised.

SUMMARY

The majority of local authority staff felt that they worked under considerable pressure, nearly one in three to the point where in their opinion they had not nearly enough time to do what they thought ought to be done. Moreover, almost one-third also assessed their level of stress and worry over their work during the last full working month, as high. Senior social workers and area management were more likely than others to feel that they worked under considerable pressure and to feel their levels of stress and worry to have been high. Social workers' assessments of their work pressures or stress levels, however, showed no marked association with the use of volunteers.

Welcoming the opportunity to offer suggestions for improving services to clients, three main priorities for both local authority social workers and probation officers emerged. These were first, changes in social work practice; secondly, more and better resources; and thirdly, a more open and flexible structure and organisation of the social services. Volunteers were rarely seen as a means of improving services.

NOTES

1 and 2 The analysis of these questions excludes the replies of the probation sample.
3 This question was taken from the Neill *et al.* (1973) study.

12 Summary and Discussion

As a result of the present inquiry, information is now available from a national and representative sample of social workers in the statutory personal social services which indicates first, the possible incidence, scale and—in very broad terms—the scope of volunteer use in these services; secondly, how social workers themselves perceive the contribution of the voluntary worker; and thirdly, the nature of some of the factors involved.

Thus it seems that, at any one time, fewer than three in five local authority social workers with caseloads are probably using the services of volunteers for their clients. Of those who are not working with volunteers, the great majority once did so. Most social workers, therefore, have present or past experience of one kind or another of working with volunteers. Only a minority of social workers who use volunteers, however, work closely with them and have personal contact with them at every stage. The most typical relationship between professionals and volunteers in the local authority services is indirect, so that the volunteers concerned are not always in close personal contact with the social workers whose clients they help, nor under their direct guidance or supervision.

As far as can be assessed in the absence of more precise data, the use of volunteers is on a relatively small scale, most users of volunteers working with only one or two at a time for no more than one or two of their clients. It is evident, however, that volunteers undertake many types of activities for a wide range of clients. The emphasis is nevertheless on two broad categories of activity— befriending, followed by practical forms of help—undertaken mainly, though not exclusively, for clients who are elderly or physically handicapped. The scope of volunteer activities, therefore, follows fairly conventional lines.

In almost every aspect of involvement with volunteers, the probation service contrasts sharply with the local authority service. There is a much higher incidence of volunteer use by probation officers, seven in ten of whom work with them. There is also much closer personal collaboration between them. The dominant relationship is a direct one. There is more personal contact at every stage and most volunteers work directly under the probation officer's guidance. The activities of volunteers in the probation service are less concentrated on practical tasks. Befriending activities on the other hand, are more evident than in the local authority services, as are tasks that require special skills and—markedly so—counselling types of help. From the evidence of this inquiry, however, the scale of volunteer use appears to be proportionately no greater, perhaps even smaller, than in the local authority services.

This contrast does not arise, apparently, as a result of any fundamental differences between the two services in the attitudes of social workers to working with volunteers, or in their experiences of so doing. Those who do use volunteers have a consistently favourable view of them, while those who do not rarely express any explicit disapproval. The main reasons for doing without volunteers are said to be organisational factors affecting the supply of suitable volunteers and, for the probation sample in particular, the smallness of caseloads and the special circumstances of their clients. Among the users, a relatively high proportion felt that voluntary workers positively helped them with the cases concerned; had no unfavourable experiences to recount and, though less so for probation officers, considered that volunteers saved their time.

This does not mean that working with volunteers is not without its problems. Those most often cited were the extra time, effort and work involved for professional staff in using volunteers, and the difficulties that arise because of what was said to be the volunteers' limitations in skill and experience; their unreliability and lack of commitment, as well as an unrealistic grasp of the nature of some of the problems they encounter. Moreover, former users of volunteers were much more frequently critical on all these counts than present users, or than those without any experience at all. The greatest reluctance to use volunteers, therefore, may be among the former users.

Substantial minorities, however, of users and non-users alike, see no disadvantages of any kind. Among those who do, the disadvantages seem, on balance, to be outweighed by the advantages. The most important advantages, evidently, particularly for probation officers and former users, are those which stem from the very nature of voluntary work itself—the volunteer's gift of time and service. This unique contribution is believed to be intrinsically different from the services the professional has to offer. It is not, however, the main reason given why volunteers are used—this simply being the tangible benefits they bring to clients and social workers—but it takes first place among the advantages listed. Most social workers, especially in the probation service, thus subscribe to a belief in the value of the volunteer's unique contribution.

Even so, social workers—whether or not they use volunteers—generally favour, in theory and in practice, the drawing of boundaries between the respective functions of the professionals and the volunteers. They define these by distinguishing the tasks for which professional training, qualifications and experience are considered necessary. For users and non-users of volunteers alike, these tasks are associated mainly with the practice of casework, as this is commonly understood. Casework, in the opinion of the profession, calls either for a degree of skill, understanding and experience which most volunteers are felt not to have, or entails responsibility and accountability—often of a statutory kind—that should not or cannot be shared. Probation officers, however, are more frequently inclined than local authority workers to feel that volunteers may cross these boundaries if they have the appropriate qualities and skills.

Thus it seems that for most social workers casework marks the boundary between themselves and volunteers. This is perhaps explained partly by the recent professionalisation of social work and by the fact that most social workers regard casework as their primary activity. There is also the attempt to establish a knowledge base for the profession by using the development of casework and casework theory (Heraud, 1970). This largely serves to differentiate social work from other more general social services and is frequently offered to justify the claim that social work is a profession. However, in as yet unpublished studies[2] comparatively few local authority social workers, when discussing their casework, referred to any specific theory or theories derived from their professional training, or gave the impression that their casework activities were based on any identifiable theoretical assumptions. This suggests that casework is not always practised as an applied science. Nevertheless, it is thought to lie at the heart of social work as a profession. For this reason, if for no other, volunteers are generally excluded from it.

TWO MODELS

In practice, probation officers would seem to have a less exclusive approach to the involvement of volunteers in casework situations. Indeed, differences in the ways social workers and volunteers work together in the two services suggest that two distinct models of volunteer use have, according to circumstances, developed in the statutory services. Each of these places a different emphasis on the role of the volunteer.

In the one model, volunteers are used mainly for carrying out tasks which the professionals feel ought to be done, but which they themselves cannot or should not do and which, without voluntary help, would not be done.

The role of the volunteer in these instances is to make up deficiencies, not necessarily only in the social services but also in the wider society, and to provide help, support and practical aid which would not otherwise be available. This is a long-established role for volunteers, as it is for many voluntary organisations and agencies. It involves some liaison between the volunteer and the professional, but does not necessarily require close collaboration between them. This is mainly because the achievement of the professional's objectives for the clients in question is not dependent on the contribution of the volunteer, the tasks undertaken by the volunteer being peripheral to the client's circumstances. In this model of volunteer use, the role of the volunteer is to supplement the work of the professional. It may therefore be termed the supplementary model of volunteer use. It is the one where the professional has relatively little control over the volunteers and also little dependence upon them.

The second model is where volunteers are used on tasks which assist the completion of casework objectives, and where some form of close partnership is essential. Here the activities of social worker and volunteer may be different and separate but they work together. The tasks then performed by the volunteer are what may be termed 'core' tasks, more central to clients' lives. They are integrated with those performed by the professional, and complement each other. Thus, the role of the volunteer in this context is to complement the work of the professional. It may thus be termed the complementary model. In it the professional has a relatively large measure of control over the volunteers, but is more dependent on them.

It is the supplementary model which predominates in the local authority services, and the complementary model in the probation service. As we have seen, however, the predominance of one model by no means precludes the development of the other within the same service or, indeed, the use of both models by the same individuals for different situations.

These models of volunteer use should not be confused with the types of relationship that have developed between the voluntary and the statutory services, as discussed in the Personal Social Services Council (PSSC) Report on Voluntary Social Services Manpower Resources (Webb *et al*. 1976).[3] In the present inquiry, the emphasis is on the relationships which have evolved between the professional and the voluntary worker in the statutory services, and it is to these that the two models of volunteer use relate.

The models are more complex than they may appear at first glance, having several dimensions which only further study, perhaps incorporating the interaction between statutory and voluntary provision, would illuminate. Nevertheless, the tentative exploration of some of these here may serve to illustrate factors underlying the use of volunteers in the statutory services and elsewhere, which need to be taken into account when considering policy and practice.

The supplementary model of volunteer use seems to be more closely associated with a scarcity of resources, including personnel, or with situations where there may be some conflict as to how and for whom such resources as are available should be used. The complementary model, on the other hand, seems to be more closely associated with some ambiguity in the professional's relationship with the client. A degree of role conflict is present which, in so far as it impedes the fulfilment of the professional's task, creates the need for a neutral agent, such as a volunteer.

Each model would also seem to differ in the extent of its application. The supplementary model has, perhaps, wider application. Hence there may be greater coverage of diverse personalities, concerns, interests and commitments, and thus a wider basis for potential recruitment. There is less need for stringent criteria for the selection of volunteers. The peripheral nature of the tasks, however important for the individuals concerned, also means a potentially wider coverage of clients. Furthermore, the demand on the professional's time and effort is minimal, since the professional is required to supply 'work', rather than to employ 'labour'.

The complementary model has, it would seem, narrower application, though this need not necessarily mean small scale schemes. It requires more care in the selection of volunteers, in the choice of client, and in the matching between them. The nature of the commitment may have a more limited, though still strong, appeal to potential volunteers so that they may be drawn from a narrower field, as indeed the clients too may be. The demands on the professional's time and effort are greater, the professional in this model being a direct 'employer' of voluntary 'labour', exercising more control and supervision generally. The investment of professional capital is much greater, therefore, in the complementary, than in the supplementary, model of volunteer use.

Yet another dimension that would merit further study is the degree of discretionary behaviour available to volunteer and client in each model. In the supplementary model, for example, each party would seem to have a wide field of discretionary action in the development of the relationship between them, since no deep commitment is required, though it may well arise. Indeed, as the Hadley and Webb study (1975) shows, several alternative types of relationship between volunteers and clients may develop. This suggests that volunteers in the supplementary model—and clients, too, for that matter—may feel freer and find it easier 'to be themselves'. Volunteers are also less likely to identify with professional behaviour, or with that of the relevant service. Relationships generally may have more expressive functions. On the other hand, the risks of volunteers proving to be unreliable or inefficient are perhaps greater in this model, since professional support is weaker. The consequences, however, when things go wrong, may not be as serious as in the complementary model.

In the latter model, volunteers and clients appear to have a smaller area of discretionary behaviour available to them. This is mainly because the development of a personal relationship at a relatively committed level of feeling and responsibility is necessary for the task on hand. In this complementary model, however, the volunteer may tend to identify his or her behaviour with the objectives of the relevant service, so that relationships may be more instrumental, being the means by which these objectives may be achieved. The risks of things going wrong, while perhaps to some extent safeguarded by professional support, are of a different order, and the disappointments and upsets which arise may have more severe consequences.

There is also the fact that each model has different implications for the status and social identity of the two parties concerned. The supplementary model, for example, tends to accentuate and the complementary to blur, the boundaries which define the respective roles of volunteers and professionals. Moreover, in the former model, professional and voluntary workers would seem to preserve their respective autonomy and independence, even though for volunteers this means, perhaps, that they are kept relatively firmly in their place in relation to their status position (as defined by the nature of the tasks they do) in the social services hierarchy. Both keep their distance and their separate identities intact. In the complementary model, a state of interdependence is created between the professional and the voluntary worker, the volunteer's status being elevated nearer to that of the professional (hence, the 'accredited voluntary associate' of the probation service), though the professional still has the main say. Their closeness is associated with shared aims and values and with a 'sharing' of their identities.

Finally, the social function of each model may be more far-reaching than is generally realised. Each typifies a different way of reconciling two apparently conflicting 'systems' of expressing concern for others—on the one hand, professionalism and paid service, and on the other, 'voluntaryism' and the free act of giving. The relationship between these two systems is by no means a stable one, since it is sensitive to changes in the social and political climate and to fluctuations in public opinion. This is partly because each system of help—originating at different periods of history and of social and economic development—reflects fundamentally different values. These are the subject of continuing argument and contro-versy, not least in the field of social welfare, where professionalism may be attacked for its 'false mystiques', and voluntaryism—parti-cularly of the more traditional kind—similarly, for having outlived its usefulness or its efficiency. Though such matters lie outside the scope of the present inquiry, it would seem important in any further study of volunteer use, and of the models that have developed, to consider the nature of the social relationships involved, the values and beliefs that underlie them and the social context in which they occur.

DIFFERENT CIRCUMSTANCES

It must be emphasised that neither model should be regarded as superior to the other, since neither has been objectively evaluated. Each would seem to have evolved as an appropriate response to different circumstances relating to the background and development of voluntary help in each service and its respective organisation, structure and function. Though the comparative study of these was outside the scope of the present inquiry, it seems important to consider, nevertheless, some of the factors that may have influenced the shape of things.

One important factor, so it seems, underlying the development of different models of volunteer use in each service is that, in the local authority service, there appears to be much greater reliance on working through voluntary organisations—traditionally the 'providers and users of volunteers' (and particularly so for many of the client groups served by the local authority social services)—than applies in the probation service (Aves, 1969). By contrast, there has been a much greater emphasis in the latter service since the Home Office circular of November 1965, on the direct recruitment, selection and training of volunteers by probation officers themselves (Reading, 1967).

It is true that, since 1972, the injection of special funds into the probation service to 'stimulate the involvement of individual volunteers and voluntary organisations' has given greater emphasis to the part played by the voluntary agencies—such as in the work of the National Association for the Care and Rehabilitation of the Offender (NACRO) (Cmnd 6590, 1976). This new emphasis, however, has not appeared to work to the detriment of the individual volunteer's contribution and, indeed, the Seebohm and Aves Committees each hoped that some such simultaneous development would arise. In the local authority services, however, such expansion in the use of individual volunteers as may have occurred is still not so important an element as the continuing reliance on the voluntary organisations and agencies.

A second factor is, perhaps, associated with the organisation and structure of each service. In the probation service for example, the Home Office itself at first stimulated, and later actively encouraged, the widespread use of volunteers in probation and after-care in ways conforming to the complementary model. Things were further influenced by the nature of the controls that the Home Office exercises over the probation service and by its establishment, through 'circulars, instruction and inspection' of common methods and standards of working (Butterworth, 1972). No comparable controls or influence apply to local authority social services departments. Moreover, in the probation service the management structure is such that seniority is not so markedly associated, as in the local authority services, with the giving up of caseloads, or with such changes in their size or composition as to lead to any noticeable fall in the use of volunteers.

A third factor, which may also influence different types of volunteer use, relates to the function of each service. There are for example, important differences in caseload composition, in casework objectives and in the relationships between social workers and clients resulting from the connections which bring them together. Local authority social services departments cover a wide range of referrals initiated by the clients themselves. The clients of the probation service have usually become so compulsorily, as a result of legal proceedings.

The Butterworth Committee (1972), for example, in its evaluation of the jobs of probation officers and local authority social workers, saw a distinction between casework situations where the main objective is to influence clients' attitudes and behaviour, and those where the greater need is for emotional support and practical help. In the Committee's view, the latter situation was more frequent in the local authority services, as far as the work of the main-grade social workers is concerned. Though, in practice, these distinctions may become blurred, the evidence of the present inquiry is consistent with the Committee's view. A relatively high proportion of referrals to social services departments for example, consists of physically handicapped and elderly people, for whom the greater need is seen as the kind of support and aid that the Committee had in mind. This emphasis noted by the Butterworth Committee, in the work of the local authority social worker, is also reflected in the composition of caseloads, particularly those of the unqualified fieldworkers and social work assistants. One result, as far as can be assessed, is a bias in voluntary help towards befriending and practical activities, mainly for elderly and physically handicapped clients.

Presumably, however, this arises largely because the perceived needs of the clients in question are met, in some way, by the supply of suitable volunteers, an important source of which (though this could not be verified in the present inquiry) is almost certainly the voluntary organisations most active in these fields, and on which local authority social workers appear often to rely.

In contrast to the comparatively wide range of social needs represented in the caseloads of local authority social workers, and the type of social work they generate, the work of the probation service is, in its nature, more highly specialised. There is also, according to the Butterworth Committee, a greater emphasis in the probation service than in the local authority services on helping or persuading clients to modify their attitudes, expectations and behaviour. At the same time, there is the need to maintain supportive relationships with a wide range of clients who are trying to re-establish themselves. Indeed, it was with such clients that voluntary help in the After-care Service began (Barr, 1971). Casework objectives are, broadly speaking, to prevent further offences and it is to the achievement of these objectives that the use of volunteers in the probation service is mainly directed, partly in the belief that volunteers may be able to establish the kind of relationship with clients that is sometimes difficult for the professional, given the probation officers' identification with the courts. Close association between probation officers and volunteers arises, however, not only in order that the task of each in relation to casework objectives may be integrated, but as part of a system of regular supervision and contact with clients by the probation officer. The probation officer is held responsible for the work done by a volunteer; and for cases derived from the courts, the probation officer is ultimately accountable to the courts.

This conjunction of circumstances, which appears to have shaped the development of two models of volunteer use, may not be unique, and other factors may assume greater importance for the future. As things stand, however, it is difficult to assess future developments, partly because the models which have evolved seem to be the most appropriate ones for each service, given their respective structures and functions. Some continuity, at least in the short term, would seem probable for local authority services, particularly in the light of the data obtained in this study. These suggest that there may be certain rigidities introduced into the situation by the division of labour and the distribution of clients generally between staff of different designations.

DESIGNATION, CASELOADS AND THE USE OF VOLUNTEERS

Two factors seem to have a decisive influence on the extent to which social workers in the local authority services use volunteers, irrespective of which model of volunteer use they adopt.

The first of these is their designation. As we have seen, as social workers rise in the hierarchy and assume positions of seniority and management in area offices, so their casework responsibilities change. Increasing seniority is associated either with the giving up of caseloads altogether, or else with considerable reductions in caseloads and changes in their composition. The result is that much smaller proportions of social workers in senior and management posts use volunteers, though the majority once did so. It is true that the picture, here, may change in the coming years, since social services departments are beginning to appoint social workers as 'senior practitioners' or the equivalent—senior grade workers without management responsibilities. Moreover, the profession itself sees the quality of social work being improved by encouraging social workers to remain in direct practice for longer periods (BASW 1977).

At the moment, however, the evidence suggests that the use of volunteers marks an intermediate stage in the career history or 'status passage' of those social workers who are making their way through the hierarchy. Social workers who have never worked with volunteers, for example, tend to represent more of the newer recruits to social work; social workers who formerly used volunteers tend to represent more of those with the most experience in social work, as do those in senior management positions.

The more experienced social workers who, by reason of their senior status and responsibility, exercise an important influence on social work practice, are thus less likely than others to be directly involved with volunteers. More important, however, is the fact that, though they may advise and recommend volunteer use, their influence is more often by precept than by example. This means first, that professional support from the more senior and qualified workers may not be available to volunteers. Secondly, in so far as their advice is based on their former rather than their current experience, it will in many ways relate to the past. The ideas they hand on may be more 'conventional' than 'innovatory', limiting, if anything, the prospects of change. Any new developments in the use of volunteers arising out of the actual experiences of those who work with them are more likely to be due to the less practised social workers.

But the potential for innovation of the less experienced may itself be restricted by a second important factor—the way cases are distributed between different groups of social workers, particularly according to designation and qualifications.

The findings of the present inquiry show clearly that the use of volunteers—especially on the lines of the more conventional, supplementary model—is determined by the size and composition of caseloads, and particularly by the representation of elderly and physically handicapped clients in these caseloads.

Not only are these two client groups much more likely to be found in the caseloads of the unqualified and less experienced staff, particularly social work assistants, but they have the highest propensity to be helped by volunteers, and are considered as the most suitable groups for voluntary intervention. Yet they also happen to have relatively low 'status' in the preferences of local authority social workers, most preferring to work with children and with families. Thus, clients of lower status, as seen by social workers, tend to be allocated to the lower ranks of social work personnel, including volunteers. This takes for granted that elderly and physically handicapped people need less skilled help. This assumption has yet to be verified, but it clearly underlies the prevailing system of caseload management.

One factor on which the findings of the present inquiry are necessarily inconclusive is relevant to this assumption. It concerns the hopes and ideas of social workers themselves about their search for self-fulfilment through their work and the nature of the rewards that they derive from their relationships with clients. Though these questions could not be explored in depth in the present inquiry, our evidence nevertheless suggests that a principal reward in working with clients is the feeling of having contributed in some way to bringing about a change for the better in the client's circumstances. Such experiences serve to confirm social workers' beliefs in their capacity to help others and to sustain their earlier hopes of finding work where they would feel useful and valued.

The importance of these satisfactions is that it is possible that some clients come to have a special meaning for social workers because working with them proves to be more rewarding—in the terms described—than does work with other clients. The significance of their rewards, however, is probably greater, given the pressures and demands of their workloads as revealed in the present inquiry, and of the conditions of the work setting in local authority services as described in the Butterworth Report (1972). The Committee's findings (which relate to local authority, probation and hospital social work services) conclude for example, that in the local authority services 'there is less certainty about the objectives of the service, or how to judge its effectiveness'; that the 'open-ended commitment' of local authority social work 'produces a conflict between the need to achieve as wide a coverage as possible from the resources available, and the desire to give a high quality service'; and that social workers are faced with a 'potentially insatiable and unending demand for their services' which, in some workers, 'generates a continuing sense of uncertainty about the direction and success of their work'. For these reasons, perhaps, local authority social workers were found to have lower job satisfaction than probation officers, particularly in the degree of autonomy in their work and in their opportunities to influence the composition of their caseloads and the pace of work.

It is not inconsistent, therefore, that when asked for suggestions as to how services to clients might be improved, volunteers were rarely mentioned by respondents in the present inquiry. Far greater emphasis was given to other measures and particularly to professional matters relating to the practice of social work. This suggests that there may be less potential for the development of more or closer collaboration between volunteer and professional, or for other forms of innovative activities, where the basic conditions under which social work is practised are in some disequilibrium, or where the 'struggle to survive' is dominant.[4]

First, such conditions may make social workers more dependent for their satisfactions on the more rewarding aspects of work with clients which, in their view, may well make voluntary intervention less welcome or less appropriate. Secondly, such conditions hardly favour the development of a model of volunteer use which, because of the close supervision and control of the volunteer by the professional, makes a greater demand on the professional's time and effort. As the Aves Committee points out, anxieties relating to the time and manpower required to make effective use of volunteers are sometimes greater in social workers' minds than are the possible effects on their professional standing or on their clients, of using volunteers, should things go wrong. In the present inquiry, nearly one in three felt that they worked under considerable pressure and could not do their work as they felt it ought to be done.

It is believed that the employment of volunteer organisers, or other persons with delegated responsibility for volunteers would help to relieve some of these anxieties and at the same time improve the standards of work (see, eg., Goldberg, 1970; Darvill, 1975; Aves, 1976; Volunteer Centre, June 1976). It is early days yet, but the indications so far, judging from information obtained in the present inquiry, are that, though such a member of staff does take on some of the duties of recruiting and organising volunteers and may influence the ways in which they are used, this does not necessarily result in a higher incidence of volunteer use. Moreover, it also tends to reinforce the supplementary model of volunteer use, indirect relationships between professionals and volunteers being more frequent, if anything, in area offices where a volunteer organiser or other delegated person is employed.

POLICY OPTIONS

It is in the light of these factors and of the type and scale of volunteer use, as revealed in the present inquiry, that the feasibility of policies aimed at achieving a higher recruitment of voluntary workers in the statutory sector, or of increasing the scope of their activities, needs to be considered. It may be unrealistic to assume that once social workers become convinced of what might be achieved through voluntary help, and are more receptive to what volunteers have to offer, this would necessarily lead to an increase in the demand for volunteers and a widening of their activities.

The findings of the present inquiry do not support the view that the numbers of volunteers could be significantly increased in the immediate future if there were 'changes in fundamental attitudes' (Darvill, 1975), or if social workers were trained in new skills. On the contrary, the evidence suggests that if there are limiting factors, then these derive less from the attitudes or lack of skills of the individuals in the profession than from the effect of the present system of the organisation and management of social services departments on the practice of social work.

Three features of this system are particularly relevant in the present context. First, the kinds of tasks that social workers are expected to undertake are determined largely by forces external to them. Social workers are not free to practise as they wish. They are, for the most part, employees of large-scale organisations, subject to rules and regulations and ultimately to lay authority. The problem of their accountability is itself a constraining influence on the use of volunteers.

Secondly, though social work has become increasingly important, to the point of becoming 'one of the major welfare institutions in modern society' (Heraud, 1970), there is within the profession, in particular since the unification of the statutory services, considerable uncertainty about the meaning of social work and how it should be defined, and considerable diversity in and dispute about method and approach. Since, as discussed in Chapter 1, the roles of professionals and volunteers within social work are interlinked, a lack of clarity inevitably also applies to the meaning of voluntary work in the statutory services and to the place of the voluntary worker. Indeed, the clarification of their roles and their relationships was considered by the Birch Committee (1976) as likely to emerge only as 'the professionals themselves acquire a firmer identity through training'.

Thirdly, there is the structure of the labour force in social work. Management and administrative levels recruit their staff mainly from the most skilled, experienced and qualified social workers, most of whom, as they assume these positions, no longer practise social work. By contrast, those in the field—the great majority of all social work staff—are recruited mainly from the untrained. The use of volunteers is thus more influenced by the untrained than the trained.

The promotion and development of voluntary activities, though based on the belief that these will bring much needed benefits to all concerned, do not always allow for the above factors upon which the viability of new policies and programmes utlimately depends. Changes in attitudes would need to be far reaching to overcome these factors and to take account of social workers' feelings about their place and prospects in the professional hierarchy and would imply major changes in the organisation and management of social work itself.

A more widespread and effective use of volunteers is, in discussion, often made contingent on changes in the training of social workers. Though, as far as we know, such changes have not yet occurred, one approach might concentrate on the kinds of skills which would encourage the development of new resources in the community. Another would emphasise the role of social workers as 'enablers' within a large team, to include volunteers. Newly trained recruits to social work, however, may find, as do some of their contemporaries in teaching, that it is sometimes difficult to put fresh ideas into practice where structural conditions remain unchanged.

Some degree of structural change would arise if there was a major development in the number of career-grade posts. Even so, the use of volunteers by those who occupy such posts is not likely to increase unless their caseloads—in size and composition—lend themselves to the use of volunteers.

Fourthly, as Ian Bruce cautions (Volunteer Centre, June 1976), any undue pressure by the statutory services to turn to volunteers only because of the shortages of staff and other resources as a result of present economic difficulties, may lead 'to the wrong decisions and to the wrong strategy'.

In our opinion, whether significantly more volunteers could or should be used in the statutory sector, and what the scope of their activities should be, are open questions. There are no precise methods for measuring, on an objective basis, either the demand or the supply factors, or for assessing how appropriate to the circumstances are the present incidence and scope of volunteer use in the local authority services. Indeed, there is only one indisputable indicator of the future demand for volunteers in the statutory sector. This is the nature of the demographic changes that may occur over the coming decades (OPCS Monitor, 1976).

These changes in population structure, resulting, for example, in an increase in the numbers of elderly people, are likely to be reflected in the patterns of referrals to social services departments and, consequently, in the composition of caseloads. To the extent that these caseloads may contain higher proportions of elderly people than they do now, so an increasing proportion of social work staff may be expected to have elderly clients in their caseloads. On the basis of the findings of the present inquiry, this factor alone may be assumed to raise the demand for volunteers. Whether it will also raise the numbers used by local authority social workers is less certain.

This does not necessarily close the policy options, however, since further developments in the use of volunteers need not depend on the statutory sector. First there are the voluntary organisations, which already recruit and supervise volunteers for the statutory services and which, as the PSSC Report shows, 'account for a substantial and diverse body of social welfare provision'. Their role—both traditional and innovatory—may assume greater importance now that the expansion in the statutory services, which followed their reorganisation, has ceased. But here, too, there are certain built-in limitations. Fieldworkers in the voluntary sector are employed on a much smaller scale than in the statutory services, according to the PSSC estimates. Also, where professional workers are employed, it may be assumed that structural and organisational factors, as well as the nature of the service given, will exercise some influence in the voluntary, as in the statutory, sector on the incidence and scope of volunteer use.

Secondly, there may be greater potential in the whole important area of self help and community involvement. Here, voluntary activity, particularly where it is autonomous, is the most far reaching, since it incorporates the spontaneous, informal response to immediate needs, as well as the long-term commitment to social and political objectives (e.g. Gulbenkian, 1973; Forester, 1976; Thomas, 1976). Here, it also would seem that, despite the growing intervention of the profession, the links with the professional are weaker—if they exist at all. Thus the constraints associated with professional services are less likely to influence the outcome. In any case, as social workers themselves would agree, the ascendency of social work as a profession does not mean that it has an exclusive claim on meeting 'human need', particularly since the definition of social work skills is still not very precise or clearly understood.

Economic recession also gives new significance to the respective roles of professional and voluntary workers, particularly if, as the areas of professional activity are reduced with the cuts in social provision, the demand for volunteers grows. There are signs of growing pressures—as in the messages from ministers and shadow spokesmen, and special features in and on the media. Moreover, the PSSC Report contains the categorical statement that, from the point of view of the manpower of the social services, it is the 'fieldwork volunteers' who are 'a direct alternative to paid workers for the voluntary organisations and for the personal social services taken as a whole'.

Important questions of principle, however, are raised by such statements. Clearly volunteers should not be used to do what paid workers are normally supposed to do, and professional workers should not support practices which might undermine standards. Any partnership, therefore, between professionals and volunteers in the statutory or the voluntary sector and designed to improve the conditions and quality of life of individuals, groups or the community at large, will, in the present economic climate, need to be based on a common standpoint and a common aim. Taking into account the fact that, in our view, there are no fixed or settled roles for either professionals or volunteers and that any definition of the roles must be transient, this aim can only be to ensure the proper use of their respective contributions and a corresponding standard of service.

NOTES

1 Excluding residential social workers and those working in day centres, sheltered workshops and similar establishments, and also professional social workers in local authority departments other than those of the social services.

2 Information derived from an interim discussion of the first four (out of eight) studies of local authority social services departments, or their equivalent: DHSS sponsored research, in conjunction with the Northern Ireland DHSS and the Scottish Social Work Services Group, under the joint direction of Professors Parsloe and Stevenson. The remit of the studies is to examine the task of the social worker in the local authority (or its equivalent) and the implications for social work education. To be published by Allen and Unwin in 1978 or 1979.

3 In the PSSC Report, voluntary provision is defined as a supplement, where it is 'similar to and essentially an extension of work being done in the statutory sector'; a substitute where it is the 'sole main form of service'; and a complement where it represents 'a specialist service not available through the state services', but 'meshed closely with statutory provision'.

   Clearly there is some overlapping in the types of relationships that have developed between voluntary and statutory services and between voluntary and professional workers. There are, however, important differences, not the least being that the voluntary agency functions at a different level from that of the individual volunteer. In any case, the present inquiry did not cover all types of volunteer activities, but only those where there was some link with the professional social worker. For this reason, any volunteers working independently of the professional through the kinds of voluntary organisations covered in the PSSC study are excluded from the present inquiry and are not covered in the models of volunteer use suggested here.

4 See note 2.

Appendix I The Use of Volunteers in the Voluntary Sector

INTRODUCTION

It had always been the intention of the present inquiry to include professional social workers employed in the voluntary sector. In the event, it proved impossible to obtain a sample of such workers which could in any way be regarded as representative and comparable with that drawn from the local authority services or the probation service. This was because, at the time of the inquiry, professional workers employed by voluntary organisations throughout the country could not have been located without extensive and time-consuming investigations.

The absence of data on the voluntary sector, in this and other respects, has been emphasised by Webb, Day and Weller (1976) in their study of Voluntary Social Services for the PSSC. They point out that a comprehensive list of all voluntary agencies, including those working in the personal social services field, does not exist. The PSSC study encountered the same problem as we did in the present BASW inquiry—the absence of an adequate sampling frame. In spite of the fact that all their efforts were centred on acquiring a sample of social workers working exclusively in the voluntary sector, and despite the substantial size of the sample eventually investigated, the authors still do not feel able to claim representativeness for this sample. Their findings, nevertheless, are based on information derived from forty-four organisations employing, on their estimates (and not counting the other categories of staff included), between 3,200-4,200 fieldworkers.[1]

As their method of approach, Webb *et al.* wrote in the first instance to voluntary organisations which were national in scope. In the present inquiry, we approached 34 nationally based voluntary organisations in this way and asked for their co-operation. Only 13 of these, however, proved eligible in the sense that they employed social workers in the sample areas, or agreed to help.[2] The organisations in question covered some 65 local offices in the sample areas and 145 professional staff from which a sample of 109 social workers was drawn. Of these, 74 (69 per cent) responded favourably to the inquiry, returning their questionnaires duly completed.

On the basis of the Webb *et al.* estimates of fieldworkers employed in the voluntary sector, the 74 social workers who participated in the present inquiry are thus only a very small proportion of the total possible number. Moreover, they are not, for the reasons given, in any way representative of those employed in voluntary organisations. Nor is it at all possible to generalise from their age, sex or other characteristics, or from the incidence and scope of volunteer use among them.

CHARACTERISTICS OF THE SAMPLE

Designation
There was considerable variation in the description given of respondents' designation and status, reflecting no doubt the particular structure of each organisation. Thus, in one agency all respondents were described as 'group officers', each responsible for the administration of the offices as well as for their own caseloads and the supervision of other staff. In another organisation, respondents were called 'organising secretaries', did not carry caseloads, but were nevertheless responsible for the organisation of voluntary help. In yet another local office, respondents were described as 'regional social workers' who appeared to be working entirely alone, responsible for relatively large numbers of cases.

Sex, Age, Qualification and Experience
As in the local authority services, women predominated, outnumbering men by a ratio of almost two to one. There was one exception to this general tendency, however, all seventeen of the social workers in the branch or regional office of one voluntary organisation being men.

There were comparatively few respondents under the age of 25 years, while as many as one half were aged 35-54, the average age of the sample being just over 42 years, this being reflected in the relatively high proportions (nearly one-half) who had been in social work for more than 10 years. This gave an average length of experience for the sample of just over 11 years. One in three, moreover, had been in their present posts for five years or more.

In terms of social work qualifications, just under one-half were qualified social workers, proportionately slightly more, therefore, than in the local authority sample. Over two-thirds had entered social work from some other type of employment.

Use of Volunteers
The services of volunteers were, at the time of the inquiry, being used by one-half of the sample on a scale not very different, as far as it could be assessed, from that in the local authority services. In many ways it seemed similar in scope. No dominant type of relationship between the professional and the volunteer was

apparent, perhaps because of the small numbers involved.

Volunteer activities were, generally, concentrated in befriending and practical types of help. Where, however, the data referred more specifically to the last instance when volunteers were used, personal support at a deeper level than befriending was more frequently cited than practical activities.

The client groups most likely to be helped by volunteers followed rather a different order from that in the local authority sample, presumably because of the specialist nature of many of the agencies, and consequently, of caseloads. In non-specialist agencies, however, families, physically handicapped people and— surprisingly enough—cases requiring fostering and adoption were more likely to be helped than elderly people. It is not possible to know how general are these patterns of help.

Advantages and Disadvantages of Using Volunteers

Most social workers in the voluntary agencies who were using volunteers emphasised as the main advantage of doing so, the fact that volunteers offer something intrinsically different from the kind of help offered by the professional. For the non-users, however, including those with previous experience of volunteers, the main advantage was the saving that might result in the social worker's time.

Few social workers who helped with volunteers saw any disadvantages, but among those who did the most frequently cited were the volunteers' lack of skill and experience and the difficulties that arose as a consequence. These difficulties were also among the disadvantages most frequently cited by social workers who did not use volunteers.

Reasons for Not Using Volunteers

An important reason, offered by nearly one in three of the non-users, for not being involved with volunteers was that it was their agency policy not to use volunteers. Further analysis showed that, of these social workers, over one-half were employed by two agencies with this declared policy. Moreover, the majority of the social workers who referred to their doubts as to the suitability of voluntary workers—when 'the bulk of casework is a one-to-one trusting relationship'— were also employed in these agencies where volunteers were, as a matter of policy, excluded. It is not possible to assess the effect of such policies in the voluntary sector, the effect on the incidence of volunteer use, or on the attitudes of the social workers concerned.

SUMMARY

The incidence and pattern of volunteer use among professional social workers employed in the voluntary organisations cannot be discerned from the present sample of respondents. It is, nevertheless, of some interest, taking into account the type of voluntary organisation from which the sample was drawn, that whilst the scale of deployment was apparently no greater than that in the statutory services, there would seem to be some differences in the client groups helped, and in the nature of the work given.

More systematic study on a larger scale than was possible in the present inquiry is required for any realistic assessment of the role of the volunteer in the non-statutory services to be made.

NOTES

1 The Webb *et al.* definition of fieldwork subsumes 'casework, groupwork, community work and welfare rights and information workers'.
2 The central offices supplied the names and addresses of locally-based staff who were then invited to participate in the inquiry. Where staff numbered fewer than five in the local office, all were invited to take part; where they numbered more than five, every other member of staff was approached.

List of Voluntary Organisations Approached

Age Concern
British Association of Residential Settlements
British Council for Rehabilitation of the Disabled
British Red Cross
Catholic Children's Society
Central Council for the Disabled
Child Poverty Action Group
Church Army
Church of England Board of Social Responsibility
Church of England Children's Society
Dr Barnardo's
Family Planning Association
Family Service Units
Family Welfare Association
Independent Methodist Church
Invalid Children's Aid Association
Jewish Blind Society
Jewish Welfare Board
Marriage Guidance Council
Mind (National Association for Mental Health)
National Association for Care and Resettlement of Offenders
National Association for Maternal and Child Welfare
National Council of Social Service
National Council of Voluntary Child Care Organisations
National Federation of Housing Associations
National Society for the Prevention of Cruelty to Children

Royal British Legion
Royal National Institute for the Blind
Royal National Institute for the Deaf
St Mungo Community Trust
Salvation Army
Soldiers', Sailors' and Airmen's Families Association
Spastics Society
United Reformed Church

Appendix II An Analysis of Response Bias

It seemed important to consider the factors which might undermine the different response rates of social workers from different local authority areas, and also to investigate the general problem of non-response. Given that 40 per cent of the total number of social workers approached had, as it were, opted out of the inquiry, it could not be assumed that the information obtained was representative. Some check had to be made, therefore, of the respondents and the non-respondents so that the extent of the possible non-response bias could be measured, and some assessment made of the representativeness of the data obtained.

A comparison was made of respondents and non-respondents regarding three characteristics on which information was available for both groups, namely sex, job designation and membership of BASW. In the analysis, local authority social workers were distinguished from probation officers, while the staff from one local authority area, for which there was no relevant information, were excluded. The analysis showed that the main differences between the respondents and non-respondents related to job designation and BASW membership. As is shown in Chapter 9, these two characteristics are inter-related—there being a higher proportion of BASW than of non-BASW members in management and supervisory posts, the difference being particularly marked among men.

Table II.1 *Response to the inquiry according to BASW membership: local authority social workers*

Membership	Respondents	Non-respondents	Total	(% of total)
BASW members	234	87	321	16
Non-BASW members	920	750	1,670	84
TOTAL[1]	1,154	837	1,991	100

[1] Excludes the staff from one local authority.

Considered on its own, however, BASW membership (as can be seen from Table II.1) seems to have been one of the factors predisposing social workers to participate in the inquiry. True, only a small minority of the sample were members of BASW—not more than one in five—but there were proportionately almost twice as as many members among the respondents as among the non-respondents. Similarly, a higher proportion of BASW members responded favourably to the inquiry than of non-members.

There was also a tendency for the response of social workers to rise with seniority. Thus, proportionately more area officers and senior social workers took part in the inquiry compared with field-workers and social work assistants and trainees (Table II.2).

Table II.2   *Response to the inquiry according to designation:*
local authority social workers

Designation	% response	Total
Area officers and deputies	69	145
Senior social workers	65	286
Fieldworkers	56	1,242
Trainees	50	104
Social work assistants	55	214
TOTAL[1]	58	1,991

[1] Excludes the staff from one authority.

Closer analysis showed that the highest response of all came from social workers in the senior positions who were also members of BASW. Between three-quarters and four-fifths of the men who were in management or supervisory positions, for example, returned their questionnaires compared with two-thirds of those who were in similar positions but who were not BASW members. Similar differences were evident among women social workers. Thus seniority, which would seem to have favoured a higher response to the inquiry, tended, when combined with BASW membership, to have produced an even higher one. This tendency is all the more striking given that BASW membership, as such, does not seem to have influenced in any way the response rates of social workers in basic-grade positions or below.

The same two factors would seem to have influenced the higher response rates of probation officers. Though fewer of them than of local authority-based staff were members of BASW, virtually all the BASW members among them took part in the inquiry, as did all but a small minority of probation staff in senior and management positions. Moreover, there were proportionately far more proba-tion officers in such positions than was the case for the sample of local authority social workers.

It appears, therefore, that the sample of respondents contains a higher proportion of BASW members and of social workers in senior and management positions than the original sample app-roached. Since, however, in both respects the numbers involved are small, such bias as does exist may be considered as marginal.

Without knowing more about the non-respondents, there was still the risk of bias in other respects, particularly where some of the important research variables of the study are concerned. The most likely bias which may have arisen from the extent of non-response is an over-representation in the sample of social workers who use the services of volunteers, the assumption being that those with a special interest in the subject under study—the use of volunteers—would have been more strongly motivated towards participation in the inquiry. No information about the non-respondents' involvement with volunteers was available. A comparison, therefore, was made of the use of volunteers among the first group of social workers to return their questionnaires and of the use of volunteers among the second and third groups to do so. It was believed that the later respondents might be more like the non-respondents in this respect. This method is one of many which attempt to overcome the problem of non-response (Lehman 1963; Morgan 1964).

This comparison did, in fact, show small differences between the three groups of respondents. The proportions of social workers

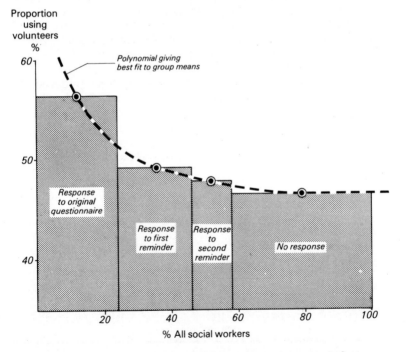

Figure II.1   *The estimated use of volunteers among non-respondents*

Table II.3   *Response to inquiry according to the use of volunteers: local authority social workers*

Use of volunteers	Response to original questionnaire	Response to 1st reminder (% of total)	Response to 2nd reminder
No	44	51	52
Yes	56	49	48
TOTAL[1]	100	100	100
(number)	(484)	(526)	(191)

[1] Excluding no replies or invalid ones.

involved with volunteers were somewhat higher among the early respondents than among the two groups of later respondents (Table II.3).

On the basis of these differences and on the assumption that social workers who did not complete the questionnaire were more akin to the most tardy of respondents than to those who were the first to reply, an estimate was made of the proportion of non-respondents who might have been using volunteers. This, as indicated in Figure II.1 and Table II.4, may have been in the region of 47 per cent. If this were so, then the proportion of social workers in the original sample approached who used the services of volunteers would be about 50 per cent. The corresponding proportion among respondents was slightly higher than this—52 per cent. If the underlying assumption can reasonably be accepted, it does not seem likely that the degree of non-response has introduced any important bias concerning the use of volunteers in the local authority sample.

Table II.4   *Estimated use of volunteers among non-respondents: local authority social workers*

Response	Number using volunteers	Total social worker sample	% using volunteers
Responding to original questionnaire	271	484[1]	56·0
Response to first reminder	259	526[1]	49·2
Response to second reminder	92	191[1]	48·2
No response	393 (estimated)	837	47·0
TOTAL	1,015 (estimated)	2,038	49.8

[1] Excluding invalid replies concerning the use of volunteers.

Appendix III Direct and Indirect Relationships with Volunteers: A Test of Consistency

It was thought important to test the consistency between the categories of volunteer use which were used in the questionnaire to identify social workers with direct or indirect relationships with their volunteers and their subsequent replies to questions concerning their contact with volunteers. A method was devised which enabled users of volunteers to be reclassified. First, a 'contact' model, based on the personal contact between social workers and volunteers was proposed, to which social workers would conform if in close touch with their volunteers at all stages—initial approach, explanation and supervision. A fifteen point scale was then designed on which, according to their answers to the questions

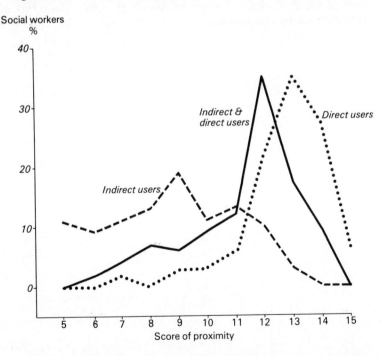

Figure III.1   *The distribution of social workers according to an index of proximity to a 'contact' model and types of relationship with volunteers*

concerning their contact with volunteers, the respondents were scored. The distribution of these scores showed the relative proximity to the model—near, intermediate and far—of volunteer users.

Two major points of interest emerged from the resulting index of proximity. First, there is clear confirmation of the earlier findings concerning the dominant patterns of social worker-volunteer relationships among local authority social workers on the one hand, and amongst probation officers on the other. The majority of local authority social workers are relatively distant from the model, compared with the probation officers, who are relatively close to it.

Secondly, if the index of proximity to the model is examined in relation to the original categories of relationship—direct, indirect and both direct and indirect—it can be seen that these three categories accord closely with the three groupings on the index of proximity (Figure III.1). Thus, the curve of the indirect users falls as it approaches the point nearest the model; that of the direct users rises very sharply towards the higher points of the scale; and that of the respondents involved in both kinds of relationship approximates to the direct users' curve. This suggests that the original classification does, after all, represent a reasonably accurate picture of social worker-volunteer relationships within the terms of reference set by this study.

Appendix IV Selection, Preparation and Training of Volunteers

Information was sought from area officers as to the arrangements, if any, for the selection, preparation and training of volunteers. Only just over one-half of area offices supplied such information which is briefly summarised below.

Selection

It has been argued that a flourishing volunteer programme is conditional on the careful selection of its volunteers, combined with their appropriate preparation and training. In the probation service for example, all volunteers are said to undergo systematic selection before becoming accredited (Clarke, 1975) and to receive systematic training; likewise in some voluntary agencies such as the Samaritans and the Marriage Guidance Council (Volunteer Centre, June 1976). We were interested to know the extent to which the local authority social services had adopted such measures and the role, if any, of the specialist appointments in these.

The data collected show that, though in the majority of area offices some selection of volunteers occurred, this was by no means on the basis of standard procedures, nor did it apply to all volunteers. But, as the Volunteer Centre (June, 1976) points out, highly developed selection procedures are hardly appropriate or necessary for many of the cases undertaken by volunteers for local authority social workers. Generally, the procedures themselves often started and ended with some form of preliminary interview, not necessarily followed by the taking up of references. There was, however, a marked association between the incidence of selection and the use of volunteers, far more social workers using volunteers where selection took place.

Moreover, selection itself was more frequent where there was a person with responsibility for volunteers. Not only was the interviewing of prospective volunteers part of the duties of these specialist officers, but their appointments seem to have had the effect of raising the number of offices where some—though not all—volunteers were selected.

Indirectly, then, specialist appointments may influence the incidence of volunteer use in so far as social workers may feel less worried about using volunteers when selection procedures, however elementary, are observed, or when they themselves do not have to spend time on such matters.

Preparation and Training

It is evident that some form of preparation and training of volunteers was being carried out in most area offices. However, this seemed to be of a rather limited nature and usually to involve only some volunteers—perhaps those new to social work. Information about the types of training schemes in operation was rather meagre and, where it was vouchsafed, somewhat imprecise. Though some respondents described what seemed to be fairly systematic training based on courses in area offices or in technical colleges, other arrangements seemed only to consist of meetings and discussions not necessarily regularly held, of induction or briefing sessions 'as and when required'. The role of specialist staff in the training schemes described was not covered by the data, though curiously enough, the more organised courses seemed to occur less often in offices where there were such appointments than where there were none. Nor was it possible to trace the possible influence of such training provisions on the incidence of volunteer use, though it may be assumed that the development of any systematic training programme would depend on continuity in the supply and deployment of volunteers.

The main impression given by the data is the informal and unstructured quality of most of the preparation and training of volunteers in the local authority services. This contrasts with the probation service, which is known to have longer established and more structured selection and training arrangements. This does not mean, however, that more highly organised procedures would be appropriate in the local authority setting. Here, the distinctions that the Volunteer Centre (June 1976) make between the 'preparation' of the volunteer at the early and more elementary stages of their involvement, and their 'training' at the more developed and complex 'end of the scale', seem particularly relevant.

Appendix V Regression Analysis

In Chapter 9 certain features of the casework situation were identified as being associated with the use of volunteers. These features were the size of the caseload and the proportion of different client groups therein. In particular, it appeared that there was a marked positive association between the use of volunteers and the proportion of elderly and physically handicapped clients in the total caseload. In order to derive a more accurate quantitative assessment of these associations, a number of regression equations were calculated from the information collected. For this purpose, the sample was divided into five size-of-caseload groups, each group being then sub-divided into two—the main fieldworker category and all other social workers. Thus ten sub-groups were distinguished, which were sufficient for purposes of the present analysis.[1]

Regression equations were then calculated with the proportion of social workers using volunteers as the dependent variable and size of caseload, the proportion of the elderly and the proportion of the physically handicapped (in the total caseload), respectively, as the independent variables. Three different forms of function were calculated: one linear and two non-linear; for the latter, a semi-log and log-inverse (or sigmoid) function were used. The regression results are summarised in Table V.1.

For each of the three relationships investigated, the regression results for the linear functions were less satisfactory than those for the non-linear ones, as is indicated by the lower value for R^2 for the linear results. It is evident that all these relationships are essentially non-linear ones, as indeed was to be expected, since it can reasonably be assumed that, in practice, there would be a maximum limit to the proportion of social workers who use volunteers, irrespective of the size or composition of the caseload. For this reason, the log-inverse function (which assumes the existence of such a maximum limit) is theoretically preferable to the semi-log function, which does not. Over the range of values covered by the sample, however, the goodness of fit (as indicated by the value of R^2) was high for both of the non-linear functions.

Taking the non-linear functions, the regressions indicate high, and statistically significant, relationships in all three cases, the goodness of fit being highest when the proportion of physically handicapped clients in the caseload is taken as the independent variable.

However, the degree of volunteer use appears to be more

Table V.1   *Regressions of volunteer use on (1) size of caseload and proportions of (2) elderly and (3) physically handicapped clients*

	Regression equation[1]	DW	R^2
(1) *Size of caseload*			
i linear	$P_v = 44.75 + 0.25\ S$	0.90	0.657
	(3.91)		
ii semi-log	$P_v = 10.35 + 13.11 \log S$	0.48	0.790
	(5.49)		
iii log-inverse	$\log P_v = 4.28 - 6.22/S$	0.47	0.797
	(-5.60)		
(2) *Proportion of elderly in caseload*			
i linear	$P_v = 38.05 + 1.54\ P_e$	1.83	0.656
	(3.90)		
ii semi-log	$P_v = 3.36 + 22.33 \log P_e$	1.67	0.702
	(4.34)		
iii log-inverse	$\log P_v = 4.46 - 4.38/P_e$	1.59	0.627
	(-3.66)		
(3) *Proportion of physically handicapped in caseload*			
i linear	$P_v = 41.73 + 0.64\ P_h$	2.04	0.811
	(5.85)		
ii semi-log·	$P_v = 6.62 + 17.19\ P_h$	2.37	0.922
	(9.72)		
iii log-inverse	$\log P_v = 4.39 - 5.49/P_h$	1.97	0.913
	(-9.18)		

[1] S = size of caseload (number of clients)
P_v = proportion of social workers using volunteers (per cent)
P_e, P_h = proportion of elderly and physically handicapped respectively in caseload (per cent)
All logarithms to base e; figures in brackets are t values of the corresponding co-efficients.
[2] DW = Durbin – Watson statistic.

sensitive to changes in the proportion of elderly clients than it is to that of physically handicapped clients, while volunteer use is least sensitive to changes in the total caseload size. The relative impacts on the degree of volunteer use of given changes in the other variables can be seen from the respective elasticities shown in Table V.2. For this purpose, the 'elasticity of volunteer use' is defined as the percentage change in Pv (the proportion of social workers using volunteers), which is associated with a one per cent change in each of the independent variables.

Thus, if Pe (the proportion of elderly clients) is increased by, say 10 per cent, this would be associated, on average, with an increase of 3.1 per cent in Pv, whereas the corresponding increase in Pv would be only 1.9 per cent for a 10 per cent increase in Ph, and only 1.0 per cent for a 10 per cent increase in S.[2]

Table V.2   *Elasticity of volunteer use based on simple regressions calculated at means of series from equations in Table V.1*

		Elasticity of P_v with respect to	
	S	P_e	P_h
1 linear	0·25	0·36	0·30
2 semi-log	0·22	0·37	0·29
3 log-inverse	0·10	0·31	0·19

A major problem in interpreting the regression results arises from the fact that the proportions of elderly and of physically handicapped clients both tend to rise as the total size of the caseload increases. For example, the increase in volunteer use as the total caseload increases (indicated in the first set of regressions in Table V.1) could reflect, to a greater or lesser extent, the influence of increasing proportions of elderly or physically handicapped clients or both rather than that of increasing caseload size *per se*. To investigate these inter-relationships further, two non-linear multiple regression equations were computed, results being summarised in Table V.3. Both equations provide a good statistical fit to the data, and both show conclusively that the major influence on the degree of volunteer use is the composition, not the size, of the caseload. The elasticity of volunteer use with respect to the combined proportion of elderly and physically handicapped clients[3] is now calculated at 0.20 (log inverse) or 0.26 (semi-log) whereas for size of caseload the corresponding elasticity is only 0.04 (log-inverse) or 0.07 (semi-log).[4]

Table V.3   *Multiple regressions of volunteer use on size of caseload and proportions of elderly and physically handicapped clients*

		Regression equation[1]	DW	R^2
1	semi-log	$P_v = -11·25 + 4·20 \log S + 15·47 \log (P_e + P_h)$ (1·76) (4·46)	2·14	0·945
2	log-inverse	$\log P_v = 4·44 - 2·53/S - 8·44/(P_e + P_h)$ (−3·30) (−6·11)	2·19	0·968

[1] Symbols as for Table V.1

NOTES

1 In principle, it would have been preferable to separate each of the five designations, but the sample was too small to allow for such a subdivision of each size-of-caseload group.

2 These percentages are based on the elasticities derived from the log-inverse regressions (as shown in the last row of Table V . 2). The semi-log results are somewhat different, but they too show the highest elasticity for the proportion of elderly clients. It should be noted that all these elasticities are calculated, for illustrative purposes, at the mean values of the variables; at other values the elasticities would be different.

3 Elderly and physically handicapped people were combined in order to avoid multi-collinearity problems.

4 Elasticities calculated at means of the variables.

Appendix VI Supplementary Tables

Table VI.1 *Caseload composition; proportion of social workers with client groups not represented in caseload according to caseload size: local authority social workers*

Client group	Size of caseload				
	1-19	20-39	40-59	60-99	100 or more
			(% of total)		
Children	31	21	19	25	61
Individuals/families	34	21	16	27	57
Fostering/adoption	50	43	32	38	64
Physically handicapped	55	29	19	9	4
Mentally ill	58	37	24	19	40
Mentally handicapped	70	39	21	24	51
Elderly	72	43	32	25	36
Other	55	32	32	40	64
TOTAL[1]	100	100	100	100	100
(number)	(138)	(237)	(226)	(159)	(56)

[1] Excluding no replies.

Table VI.2 *Caseload composition; proportion of social workers with client groups not represented in caseload according to designation: local authority social workers*

Client group	Area officers/ deputies	Senior social workers	Field workers	Trainees	Social work assistants
			(% of total)		
Children	41	22	18	21	74
Individuals/families	45	32	19	14	41
Fostering/adoption	55	44	34	44	82
Mentally ill	49	38	27	33	50
Physically handicapped	66	53	22	19	10
Mentally handicapped	82	53	32	30	44
Elderly	83	73	38	26	36
Other	75	53	33	33	59
TOTAL[1]	100	100	100	100	100
(number)	(30)	(95)	(545)	(57)	(90)

[1] Excluding no replies.

Table VI.3 *Caseload composition; proportion of social workers where client groups represent 40 per cent or more of total caseload according to caseload size: local authority social workers*

Client group	Size of caseload				
	1-19	*20-39*	*40-59*	*60-99*	*100 or more*
			(% of total)		
Children	28	16	19	16	4
Individuals/families	15	10	3	4	–
Fostering/adoption	7	4	2	1	–
Elderly	5	5	3	5	14
Physically handicapped	4	1	14	26	68
Mentally ill	3	1	2	1	3
Mentally handicapped	2	1	2	3	–
Other	6	8	6	1	4
TOTAL[1]	100	100	100	100	100
(number)	(138)	(237)	(226)	(159)	(56)

[1] Excluding no replies.

Table VI.4 Average caseload composition according to designation and qualifications: local authority social workers

Client group	Qualified				Unqualified					
	Area officers/ deputies	Senior social workers	Field workers	Total (% of total)	Area officers/ deputies	Senior social workers	Field workers	Trainees	Social work assistants	Total
Children	38	34	28	29	11	33	21	14	3	17
Individuals/families	15	14	19	18	34	17	15	23	11	15
Fostering/adoption	13	12	9	10	7	13	6	6	2	5
Mentally ill	11	9	8	9	11	5	7	5	3	6
Physically handicapped	7	9	8	8	12	11	24	19	44	27
Mentally handicapped	5	8	7	7	16	7	7	7	5	6
Elderly	3	4	8	7	6	4	11	14	25	14
Other	8	10	13	12	3	10	9	12	7	9
TOTAL[1]	100	100	100	100	100	100	100	100	100	100
(estimated number of cases)	(420)	(1,030)	(10,780)	(12,230)	(80)	(420)	(18,280)	(1,530)	(5,080)	(25,490)

[1] Excluding no replies.

Table VI.5 Average caseload composition according to use of volunteers and designation: local authority social workers

Client group	Users						Non-users					
	Area officers/ deputies	Senior social workers	Field workers	Trainees	Social work assistants	(% of total)	Area officers/ deputies	Senior social workers	Field workers	Trainees	Social work assistants	Total
Children	36	30	23	10	3	19	31	37	26	20	2	24
Individuals/ families	22	13	16	15	10	15	17	16	18	31	16	18
Mentally ill	13	9	8	3	4	7	11	6	7	7	3	7
Elderly	8	4	10	15	27	12	1	4	8	10	20	9
Physically handicapped	5	14	21	31	43	25	10	6	14	14	43	16
Mentally handicapped	4	10	7	7	5	7	9	6	6	6	4	6
Fostering/ adoption	3	10	6	6	1	6	18	15	8	5	2	8
Other	9	10	9	13	7	9	3	10	13	7	10	12
TOTAL[1]	100	100	100	100	100	100	100	100	100	100	100	100
(estimated number of cases)	(210)	(1,200)	(17,420)	(1,180)	(2,180)	(22,190)	(320)	(900)	(12,550)	(680)	(1,200)	(15,650)

[1] Excluding no replies.

Table VI.6   *Average proportions of cases according to types of
social work attention given and designation: local authority
social workers*

Type of social work attention	Area officers/ deputies	Senior social workers	Field workers (% of total)	Trainees	Social work assistants
Active, ongoing intervention	42	48	40	31	22
Mainly supportive work from social worker	36	29	36	45	50
Aid and support mainly from others	13	14	11	13	16
Assessment	4	8	10	10	11 .
Other	5	1	3	1	1
TOTAL[1]	100	100	100	100	100
(estimated number of cases)	(540)	(2,150)	(27,500)	(1,760)	(5,330)

[1] Excluding no replies.

Table VI.7   Preferences for client groups: local authority social workers[1]

Client group	Would prefer to work with	No preference	Would prefer not to work with (% of social workers)	No reply	Total (number)
Children	66	20	6	8	
Fostering/adoption	52	27	13	8	
Families	49	38	5	8	
Children before the courts	48	26	18	8	
Mentally ill	41	35	16	8	
Individuals with other problems	34	50	5	8	
Mentally handicapped	30	41	20	11	
Elderly	28	43	20	9	100
Other physically handicapped	20	55	20	9	(810)
Homeless	17	40	33	5	
Prisoners	14	50	28	10	
Adults before the courts	12	38	39	8	
Physically ill	12	56	27	11	
Blind	9	50	39	5	
Deaf	5	43	48	2	

[1] Caseload holders only.

Table VI.8   *Proportions working with preferred client groups:*
local authority social workers

Client group preferred	% with client group in caseload	% with client group representing 30% or more of caseload	Number of social workers
		(% of social workers)	
Deaf	94	59	40
Blind	90	64	73
Other physically handicapped	90	43	162
Homeless	86	78	138
Children	84	34	535
Individual with other problems	83	20	275
Mentally handicapped	83	7	243
Mentally ill	78	7	332
Fostering/adoption	76	7	421
Adults before courts	76	20	97
Elderly	75	15	227
Prisoners' families	75	15	113
Families	74	19	397
Children before the courts	70	13	389
Physically ill	50	9	97

Bibliographical References

BOOKS AND ARTICLES

Andrews, C., 'Part-time social work', *Social Work Today*, vol. 5, no. 6 (13 June 1974)

Bamford, Terence, 'Getting value for money out of the social services', *The Times* (18 May 1977)

Barr, Hugh, *Volunteers in Prison After-Care*, National Institute Social Services Library, No. 20 (Allen & Unwin, 1971)

Barr, Hugh, *Social Work Today*, vol. 3, no. 21 (25 January 1973)

Brontë, Charlotte, *Shirley* (Collins edn 1849)

Cogan, M. and Terry, J., *The Organisation of a Social Services Department—A Blueprint* (Bookstall Publications, 1971)

Darvill, G., *Bargain or Barricade?* (The Volunteer Centre, 1975)

Forester, Tom, 'Village contacts', *New Society*, vol. 38, no. 738 (25 November 1976)

Gaskell, Elizabeth, *North and South* (Everyman edn, Dent, 1854)

Goldberg, E. Matilda, *Helping the Aged*, National Institute Social Work Training Series (Allen & Unwin, 1970)

Goldthorpe, John H., 'Social stratification in industrial society', in R. Bendix and S. H. Lipset (eds), *Class Status and Power* (Routledge & Kegan Paul, 1967)

Hadley, Roger, Webb, Adrian and Farrell, Christine, *Across the Generations: Old People and Young Volunteers* (Allen & Unwin, 1975)

Halmos, Paul, *The Faith of the Counsellors* (Constable, 1965)

Hatch, Stephen, and Mocroft, Ian, 'Voluntary workers', *New Society*, vol. 40, no. 757 (7 April 1977)

Heraud, Brian J., *Sociology and Social Work: Perspectives and Problems* (The Commonwealth and International Library, 1970)

Jeffreys, Margot, *An Anatomy of Social Welfare Services* (Michael Joseph, 1965)

Jenkins, Rachel, and Aldridge, Meryl, 'BASW membership survey', *Social Work Today*, vol. 5, no. 21 (23 January 1975)

Judge, Ken, letter to *The Times* (28 March 1977)

Lehman, E. C., 'Tests of significance and partial returns to mail questionnaires', *Rural Sociology*, no. 28 (1963)

Leonard, P. 'The application of sociological analysis to social work training', *Readings in Social Administration* (Penguin Books, 1973)

Lynch, Bruce, 'Job satisfaction in social work', *Social Work Today*, vol. 7 no. 11 (19 August 1976)

Morgan, R. H., 'Non-response in postal questionnaire surveys', *Area* (Institute of British Geographers), no. 6 (1974)

Morris, Mary, *Voluntary Work in the Welfare State* (Routledge & Kegan Paul, 1969)

Neill, June E., Fruin, David, Goldberg, E. Matilda, and Warburton, R. William, 'Reactions to integration', *Social Work Today*, vol. 4, no. 15 (1 November 1973)

Neill, June E., Warburton, R. William, and McGuinness, Brendan,

'Post-Seebohm Social Services: (1) The social worker's viewpoint. Perceptions of social workers in four area offices in 1972 and 1975' (*Social Work Today*, vol. 8, no. 5 (2 November 1976)

Pearson, Geoffrey, 'Social work as the privatised solution of public ills', *British Journal of Social Work*, vol. 3, no. 2 (Summer 1973)

Reading, P., 'Extending the use of volunteers', *Social Work Today*, vol. 7, no. 4 (13 May 1976)

Scott, C., 'Research into mail surveys', *Journal of the Royal Statistical Society*, series A, no. 124 (1961)

Smith, G. and Harris, R., 'Ideologies of need and the organisation of social work departments', *British Journal of Social Work*, vol. 2, no. 1 (Spring 1972)

Thomas, David N., *Organising for Social Change*, National Institute Social Services Library, No. 30 (Allen & Unwin, 1976)

GOVERNMENT PUBLICATIONS

Classification of Occupations, 1960, Office of Population Censuses and Surveys (HMSO, 1960)

Report of a Committee on Children and Young Persons in Scotland, Cmnd 2306 (Kilbrandon Report) (HMSO, 1964)

Report of the Work of the Probation and After-Care Department 1962-65, Cmnd 3107, Home Office Circulars 144/65 and 238/65

Report of the Working Party on Social Workers in Local Authority Health and Welfare Services (Younghusband Report) (HMSO 1967)

The Place of Voluntary Services in After-Care, Second Report of Working Party (Reading Report) (HMSO, 1967)

Report of the Committee on Local Authority and Allied Personal Social Services, Cmnd 3703 (Seebohm Report) (HMSO, 1968)

Young School Leavers, Report of an inquiry carried out for the Schools Council by the Government Social Survey (Schools Council Inquiry 1) (HMSO, 1968)

Report into the Work and Pay of Probation Officers and Social Workers, Office of Manpower Economics (Butterworth Report) (HMSO, 1972)

Social Services, Volunteers and the Community, by Carolyn Davies and Deborah Filson (Department of Health and Social Security, Statistics and Research, 1973)

Local Authority Social Services Departments at 30th September 1974 (S/F75/1) (Department of Health and Social Security, Statistics and Research, 6, 1974)

'Full-time teachers in maintained primary and secondary schools', *Teacher Statistics*, vol. 4, table 13 (HMSO, 1975)

Great Britain 1971 Census, Economic Activity, Part II and Part IV (HMSO, June 1975 and January 1976)

Department of Employment Gazette (HMSO 1976)

Manpower and Training for the Social Services, Report of a Working Party for the Department of Health and Social Security (Birch Report) (HMSO, 1976)

'Population projections, mid-1975 based', *OPCS Monitor*, 76/1 (Office of Population Censuses and Surveys, 1976)

Registrar-General Population Estimates, 1974 Revised, 1975 Provisional,

England and Wales, Series PP1, no. 1/2, Office of Population Censuses and Surveys (HMSO, 1976)

Report on the Work of the Probation and After-Care Department 1972-75, Cmnd 6950 Home Office (HMSO, 1976)

OTHER REPORTS

The Voluntary Worker in the Social Services, Report of a Committee jointly set up by the National Council of Social Service and the National Institute for Social Work Training (Aves Report) (Allen & Unwin, 1969)

Current Issues in Community Work (Gulbenkian Report) (Routledge & Kegan Paul, 1973)

Volunteers Accredited to the Probation Service, by A. T. Clarke (Hertfordshire Probation and After-Care Service, 1975)

Pivot, Report of a Working Party on the National Association of Voluntary Help Organisers (NAVHO) (Chairman, Geraldine M. Aves, OBE) (Volunteer Centre, 1976)

Voluntary Social Services Manpower Resources, by Adrian Webb, Leslie Day and Douglas Weller (Personal Social Services Council, 1976)

Encouraging the Community, Some Findings on the Social Services Departments' Contribution (Volunteer Centre, May 1976)

Creative Partnerships, A Study in Leicestershire of Voluntary Community Involvement (Volunteer Centre, June 1976)

Directory of Headquarters-Based Liaison Officers for Community and Voluntary Services, 1st edn (Volunteer Centre, December 1976)

The Social Work Task, BASW Working Party Report (BASW Publications, 1977)

Training Volunteer Organisers, by Kay Richards (National Institute for Social Work Papers, No. 3, 1977)

The Future of Voluntary Organisations, Report of the Committee on Voluntary Organisations (Wolfenden Report) (Croom Helm, 1977)

Index